The
Divorce
Doctor

The Divorce Doctor

Francine Kaye

First published and distributed in the United Kingdom by:
Hay House UK Ltd, 292B Kensal Rd, London W10 5BE.
Tel.: (44) 20 8962 1230; Fax: (44) 20 8962 1239. www.hayhouse.co.uk

Published and distributed in the United States of America by:
Hay House, Inc., PO Box 5100, Carlsbad, CA 92018-5100.
Tel.: (1) 760 431 7695 or (800) 654 5126; Fax: (1) 760 431 6948 or (800) 650 5115.
www.hayhouse.com

Published and distributed in Australia by:
Hay House Australia Ltd, 18/36 Ralph St, Alexandria NSW 2015.
Tel.: (61) 2 9669 4299; Fax: (61) 2 9669 4144. www.hayhouse.com.au

Published and distributed in the Republic of South Africa by:
Hay House SA (Pty), Ltd, PO Box 990, Witkoppen 2068.
Tel./Fax: (27) 11 467 8904. www.hayhouse.co.za

Published and distributed in India by:
Hay House Publishers India, Muskaan Complex,
Plot No.3, B-2, Vasant Kunj, New Delhi – 110 070.
Tel.: (91) 11 4176 1620; Fax: (91) 11 4176 1630. www.hayhouse.co.in

Distributed in Canada by:
Raincoast, 9050 Shaughnessy St, Vancouver, BC V6P 6E5.
Tel.: (1) 604 323 7100; Fax: (1) 604 323 2600

A catalogue record for this book is available from the British Library.

ISBN 978-1-84850-089-1

Cover image © Charlie Kaufman at Fresh Academy

Printed in the UK by CPI William Clowes Beccles NR34 7TL

Contents

Acknowledgements   vii

Foreword   xi

Introduction: The Impossible Fairy Tale   xiii

Part One   The Emergency Room   1
Chapter One   First Aid   3
Chapter Two   Intensive Care   25
Chapter Three Regaining Consciousness   56

Part Two   Recuperation   75
Chapter Four The Ex Files   77
Chapter Five Kids Don't Divorce   119

Part Three   Scrubbing Up for Life Apart   155
Chapter Six   Financial Fitness   157
Chapter Seven Taking Charge of Your Career   ·   173
Chapter Eight Having a Healthy Balance – Making More
                  Time for Your Life   187

Part Four   The Recovery Room   209
Chapter 9   From Conflict to Co-operation   211
Chapter 10   Wellness – the New You!   237

Resources   277

Dedicated to my parents, Doris and Stanley Kaye. Your love for and commitment to each for over 54 years is awesome. I love you both very much.

Acknowledgements

A book like this doesn't just happen. A whole chain of events must conspire in order for it to be written, and many people have contributed to its conception and its birth. It's a real pleasure to acknowledge the wonderful people who helped make this book possible so that you, my reader, can ultimately benefit from it.

Firstly, huge thanks to Michelle Pilley and everyone at Hay House for believing in the relevance of this book. I am totally privileged and honoured to be working with the best personal development publishing house in the world. Thank you so much from my heart.

Thank you to the wonderful Barbara Vesey, whose intelligent and succinct editing polished the finished article until it gleamed.

Thank you to my agent, Jaine Brent, for believing in me and my work, and to the effervescent Antony Read at UK Casting for being by my side and always encouraging me every step of the way.

Thank you to all my great teachers and influencers over the years. All of them will recognise something that they have contributed to me in this book:

Carl Rogers, Dr Thomas Gordon, The Landmark Forum, my teachers at The Coaches Training Institute and Ian McDermott at ITS, Dr Charles Hobbs, Jonathan Robinson, Dr Bruce Fisher, the wonderful Grainne O'Malley and Anthony Robbins. I have learned so much from you all, and the journey continues.

Thank you to the following people who have shown me so much love and have been a part of my life through all my ups and downs.

Top of my list are my incredible children, Carly and Alex Lipman. It's been a journey, hasn't it guys? Our decision to be a threesome has been the greatest gift of my life. In an ideal world mums and dads stay together forever, and yet the time I have had with you two alone has made me the luckiest mum in the world. Carly, I have watched you grow into a kind, fair and worldly wise young lady. I love our holidays together and how you organise me. I love that you are my very best friend and I also love it when you still need 'mummy cuddles' to make it all better. I am so proud of your work ethic and your achievements. Keep growing girl, it gets better and better.

Alex, my number one son. You and I share something so special it cannot even be named. We walk in step, we laugh at the same things and you are the most intuitive and imaginative person I know. Like your sister you too have an incredible work ethic. Both of you had to become strong independent people and you have managed it with good grace and elegance. Alex, you are an amazing writer, a fabulous actor and a complete star. With you it's always a 'Lovely Day'.

With my loving thanks to my partner, Gary Hall. You made me feel beautiful again and you never doubt my abilities. For 13 years you have encouraged me in everything I do and always wave my flag. I so appreciate that and I wish you continued success and the very best life has to offer.

My lovely Erica Gee. Our 30-year friendship is amazing, funny, loving and a constant source of learning. You were there when my marriage began, you were there when it fell apart and you have continued to be there for me through thick and thin. Your laughter and love have been a constant source of pleasure and I love you loads.

My darling Susan Moss. The wisest lady I know. You too know what it feels like to go through this experience and you also know that it's possible to get over it, grow stronger and let new love in. You are a sage and loving soul mate and I thank you so much for being in my life.

Thank you to Annie Simmonds for giving me my first 'proper' job after my divorce and remaining my playmate ever since. Thanks to Lynda and Henry Vellerman, for your patience and love even when I didn't deserve it, and for your fabulous dinners. Thank you to my wonderful cousins Gillian and Martin May, Lesley and Irving Singer, Paulette and Mark Sachon and Nigel Gee and to my brother- and sister-in-law Jeremy and Michele Kaye. You have all looked after me, supported me and I love you all so much.

Thank you to Fiona Harrold for having me on your team, for your wonderful cards and endless words of encouragement. You are my mentor and my friend.

Thank you to Andrew Rhodes at Sobell Rhodes. You are not only my financial guru and an amazing accountant; you are also my friend and the hottest networker I know. Without you the next chain of thank you's would not exist.

Thank you to Trevor Sorbie, hairdresser extraordinaire, for believing in my work and introducing me to Matthew Wright. A huge thank you to the wonderful Matthew Wright for inviting me to give advice on your show, *The Wright Stuff*. Matthew, you are passionate about helping people in rocky relationships. You are quick and clever and genuinely compassionate and I love working with you.

Thank you to Vanessa Lloyd Platt, expert family lawyer, for being a supporter of my work. You explode the myth that many people have about lawyers. You always advise clients to see me if you think their marriage can be saved or when they need emotional support during a difficult divorce. You hold the bar for integrity and justice, and I am very proud to be part of your team.

Thank you to my ex-husband Mark Lipman. I would not be the woman I am today without our divorce. I appreciate the gift of our children and the love you show them and everything I have learned as a result of our marriage and divorce.

And last but not least, thank you to my wonderful courageous clients who were willing to discover their own role in what happened and why it happened and learning that you can avoid making the same mistakes again. In this book your names, situations and circumstances have been changed to honour your privacy, and some stories are a composite of several situations. I want you to know that I am so proud of those of you who have rebuilt your relationships through our work together and equally as proud of those of you who have used the skills and tools to divorce with dignity, parent effectively, heal your hearts and learn to love again. Thank you so much for allowing me to share your journey.

Foreword

I have known Francine, first professionally and then personally, for more than ten years. She is extraordinarily gifted, and the smartest relationship and communication expert I know.

I have sent literally hundreds of people to see her over the years. All of them had one thing in common: they all needed help – and I gave them Francine's number knowing she would help them improve their lives dramatically. I have been urging her to write a book for all the people who can't get to see her personally – and here it is, and it's wonderful! You get the real Francine here – her wit and wisdom, her tough talking and her uplifting spirit.

Sadly marriage doesn't come with a user manual, and nor does divorce. Thank heavens, then, that we've got The Divorce Doctor. Francine is fascinated by people and by relationships, and has been interested in communication for as long as I've known her; she has studied it and taken innumerable courses on the subject. She walks the walk and has her own wealth of personal experience behind her. In these pages Francine shows us how the patterns and behaviours that make us unhappy and stop us having great relationships do not need to stay that way for ever.

It really is possible to have a happy divorce. I've seen Francine help people achieve it. This book is just like a session with Francine and, by the end of it, you'll know yourself a whole lot better and be equipped with the tools to move forward into your future.

Francine is wonderful, and so is this book. Good luck!

Fiona Harrold, author *The Seven Rules of Success*

Introduction:
The Impossible Fairy Tale

Once upon a time, in a far-off country called The Past, way before you and I knew what we know now, a very nice girl met an equally nice boy and they fell in 'like'. They liked each other so much that they decided to take it one step further and fall in 'even more like' (which they called love) and tie the knot. As time went by, these very nice people, just like you and me, found that they didn't feel the same as they did when 'like' had turned into 'love'. Something was missing. They began to change. Unfortunately, they forgot to tell each other about these changes.

One day they woke up together in their very nice house with their very nice children and one of them realized that the relationship wasn't working any more. One of them didn't feel the same as they used to. This revelation led the other to agree that they, too, were not as happy as they used to be. So they decided not to cause each other any more unhappiness and both of them sat down together to work out how they could still be great parents to their kids and make sure each of them had enough money to start their new lives. They decided that they both would stay friends with each other and each other's families and friends, and after a while they came up with a 'Post-marriage Master Plan' which they both agreed to follow. When all that was done and dusted, they threw a big 'Completion Party' for everyone they knew. They both invited their new partners, had a wonderful evening together, and everybody lived happily ever after.

Yeah *right!*

From where you are now, I know this sounds like an impossible fairy story. After all, how many people do you know who have ended their relationships as friends and waltzed into their new lives with ease and elegance? Probably not that many.

No one goes into marriage expecting to divorce. There was a time when you loved your partner and your partner loved you. You may still have deep feelings for your ex-partner even though your marriage is no longer viable. But this doesn't mean that you have to participate in all-out warfare. Bearing in mind that neither of you planned for this to happen, how about considering a different way of ending your old love relationship? How about becoming an example to yourself by divorcing with dignity and emerging with your sanity intact instead of becoming a warning to others about the miseries of divorce?

It's absolutely true to say that there are people who have been fabulous examples of how to divorce without drama, and most of us know of 'a friend of a friend' who spends summer holidays with their ex-partners and their children. So how do they do that? Why is it possible for some couples and not for others?

For most couples (the exceptions being in situations where violence or abuse has reared its ugly head) it has nothing to do with their specific or unique circumstances. It's simply because no one showed them how to do it differently. Until now.

From where I sit I know that it's perfectly possible to write your own happier ending, because every day I work with couples to give them the skills and tools to do just that. I watch them as they end their own private war, stop defending and justifying their positions and move towards an understanding of what happened and why it happened, to finally move forward in peace.

Welcome to My Surgery

The whole purpose of this book is to get you to a place where you can do the same. Think of it as your Divorce Handbook. It will leave no stone unturned in its efforts to get you through this phase in your life all in one piece. You are going to be in state of flux for a while yet. You can either spend every day as if you were an all-in wrestler and emerge battered and bruised, or you can drop the drama and wake up every day knowing you can *choose* your attitude to whatever happens. And I do mean 'whatever happens'. You see, it only takes one person to decide to divorce with dignity – let that person be you!

Moving towards a Drama-free Divorce

It doesn't matter how your partner behaves or what they say or do. Absolutely anyone who wants a drama-free divorce can follow the guidelines in this book and learn how to cope with the emotional and practical stages of the journey ahead. Not only that, when you realize that you have the power to take back control of your life and choose your responses to whatever happens, you will emerge from this stage in your life feeling buoyant, not bitter.

So, if you are headed in the direction of divorce, are in the process of divorce or are divorced and still recuperating, this book is for you. The reality is that your life does not stop because you are splitting up. What makes this book unique is the way it will show you how to cope in every area of your life as you go through the stages of divorce. It will give you specific prescriptions to help you heal at each stage. You will understand the symptoms that led to your relationship breakdown. You will learn ways to speed up your recovery by making clear, focused choices for your life and, ultimately, break through the disease and return to full health with your identity intact.

This book is a course of treatment that contains all the skills and strategies I have learned from some wonderful teachers with whom I have worked over the past decade. You'll learn how to manage your life, release any negative emotions and beliefs, and create lasting happiness. You'll discover how to maintain your dignity, regain your identity, communicate effectively and emerge positively when it's all over.

So if you feel like you are currently starring in the soap opera from hell, then welcome to my surgery. You have come to the right place. Pull up a chair, sit yourself down and, in the words of the great Winston Churchill, 'Let us move forward together!'

Part One
The Emergency Room

Chapter One
First Aid

Awareness	*Of the divorce disease and its impact*
Attitude	*How to lower your emotional temperature and respond appropriately*
Action	*Deciding what actions will best serve you and what actions won't*

Emergency Treatment
Till Divorce Do Us Part

Whilst it may be little comfort to you, I want you to know that you are not alone in a strange country where no one understands what you are going through.

According to the Office of National Statistics in the UK, currently one in three marriages ends in divorce. Some 3,200 people divorce each week. By any standards, that is a lot of people. If the same number of people were experiencing measles or mumps each week there would be a public outcry and the government would step in to begin an immunization programme immediately. As far as I am concerned, divorce is a 'dis-ease'. It's not a medical condition (although sometimes its impact can cause physical and mental distress), it's more a stomach-churning feeling of discomfort, a period of all-encompassing 'dis-ease' with yourself and your life, which can be as powerful as any medically recognized condition.

However, divorce will probably never be acknowledged as a 'dis-ease' even though it affects so many. The reason for this is that the word 'divorce' receives particularly bad press. It has a powerful emotional impact on most of us, because as soon as the word is uttered we know that pain is not far behind. Divorce means it's going to cost you one way or another, financially or emotionally – and usually both. We hope that if we don't say the word it will never happen to us. Let's not look at it or discuss it. I'll bet some people didn't even now how to spell the word until Dolly Parton helped us out. So how can we address its symptoms and create a long-lasting 'cure' unless we have the courage to acknowledge that it is currently affecting over 42 per cent of the population? We can't, and that's why so many people out there are doing divorce the hard way instead of receiving the right skills to show them an easier way. People are caught up in the drama of their divorce, and too many of them are left broken and bitter by the experience.

Why Is Divorce Such a Drama?

Is it because it evokes a level and depth of anger that comes from a place inside you never before discovered? Is it because you experience an incredible amount of pain that creates a toxic explosive emotion that erupts spontaneously every time your ex comes anywhere near you? Is it because the agreement from your friends and family that you are totally right and your ex is unequivocally wrong makes you dig in your heels for the battle of the century? And does all that add up to drama? You bet.

The problem is that drama of this magnitude, if allowed to run wild, always hurts the couple concerned – *and* their children. It takes over their entire lives and perpetuates a rising emotional temperature guaranteed to have some of the less scrupulous lawyers laughing all the way to the bank.

The truth is that whether you are the leaver or the 'leavee', there is no question that ending a relationship can be a roller-coaster ride of emotions. Expect the unexpected. There will be times, possibly right now, when you feel disorientated and disconnected from yourself and the world. I promise, this is perfectly normal – and if you're feeling it, you can bet that millions of others in your situation have also felt the same. It may also be that you are in that strange 'in between' place where you know that you cannot carry on in the relationship as it is right now and you really think divorce is the only answer, but maybe, just maybe, there is still something more that you could do to save your relationship.

How Can You Be Sure that You Are Really Ready for Divorce?

At this very early point in your relationship breakdown, it's important for me to state categorically that it's possible that divorce, if treated effectively in its early stages, can often be prevented. Not everyone who feels divorce 'coming on' actually gets divorced.

Many people can get over the early symptoms and live long and healthy marriages and partnerships. It's certainly true for some couples that receiving and using the right 'preventative' treatment when specific symptoms raise their heads, can work. *But that's only if you manage to spot the symptoms in the first place and you are both committed to finding a cure.*

How Do I Know If It's Really Over?

Both the leaver and the leavee will often ask this question of themselves for quite a while before, during and even after their divorce. If you want to know if it's truly over, you'll need to answer some pretty tough questions. You certainly need to be sure that you are manifesting enough of the symptoms of this disease to make divorce the only way forward. Wherever you are right now, I'd like you to answer these questions as honestly as you can.

The Symptoms of Divorce

- Are you experiencing aggressive behaviour?
- Are you experiencing physical or mental abuse?
- Have you made unacceptable personal compromises?
- Does your partner put you down, undermine or embarrass you?
- Are you able to speak openly and say what you want to say?
- Are there lies and incidents of deception?
- Are you being ignored?
- Are you experiencing guilt?
- Have you lost trust in your relationship?
- Have you existed in silence?
- When were you last intimate with your partner?
- Are you being criticized or judged?
- Does your partner abuse alcohol or drugs?
- Has your partner cheated on you?
- Are there excuses about everything?
- Have you lost interest in each other?
- Do you talk openly to each other?
- Has your partner stopped listening to you?
- What is the recurring conflict between you?
- What recurring conflict makes you put up your barriers, attack each other and end up with a stalemate?
- Are you willing to let go of this conflict and find resolution?
- If not, why not?

If you have answered yes to most of the questions above, then it's probable that your relationship has come to an end and this book will help you on your journey ahead towards divorce.

If after having looked at all the symptoms that led you to this place and for any reason, you still have even the slightest doubts, then I would urge you to answer the next seven questions before giving up on your marriage:

1. Are you sure that the difficulties in your relationship are not just a product of your own thinking and attitudes?
2. Do you understand your own 'rules' for a relationship?
3. Are you clear about what you must have in a relationship, and can you make a distinction between what you want and what you are getting?
4. Have you clearly communicated your needs to your partner in a way that they can understand?
5. Do you understand enough about your own role in this relationship to be sure that you can and will choose a better partner next time?
6. Have you tried everything – for instance, have you seen a great counsellor or divorce coach individually and together? (I have helped many couples rebuild their relationships, so I know that it's possible.)
7. While it's important that you don't stay in your relationship out of fear or dependency (and you certainly must not tolerate any form of abuse), have you considered the consequences of divorce on every area of your life – and can you see yourself coping with them?

Having answered all of the above, are you absolutely sure that you still want to go ahead with your break-up?

Very few divorcees sail through this experience unscathed. Fewer still fall instantly into the arms of a perfect partner who is waiting in the wings to scoop them up (and their children) and take them off to 'Happily Ever After Land'.

I'm not saying this to frighten you, simply to point out that during difficult times it's easy to think that the grass is bound to be greener outside your relationship. This is not always the case. All I am saying is be as sure as you possibly can be that you are doing the right thing for you. If you have any doubts whatsoever, get in touch with me so we can look at what can be done to save your marriage.

The Prognosis

If you are quite sure that separating is right for you, then you should know that there may well be storms on the horizon. For those men and women who go on to contract full-blown 'divorce-itis', the immediate prognosis can be painful and may include a few complications along the road to full recovery.

> However, therein lies the good news: Divorce is a disease from which anyone can completely recover and go on to lead a happy and fulfilling life.

Not only that but, because divorce happens over time, many people are compelled to become more self-reliant, more creative and resourceful and in the long run more knowledgeable about themselves as well as being more understanding of others. With the right 'prescriptions' (drug free, of course), designed specifically for you, there is absolutely no reason for you to experience being in this place ever again.

People recovering from a debilitating illness will tell you that there is a process that you must go through as you rid your body of the toxins that led to its breakdown. Some people try to cut corners or take short cuts, and very often set back their healing by days or weeks. Divorce is a bit like that. The more you resist it, the harder your road to recuperation.

Some days you'll feel fighting fit, your strength seems to have doubled and you are sure you are getting over it. The very next day something or nothing happens and you feel more weak and vulnerable than ever before. Learning how to manage yourself through this time is the only way towards a speedier recovery.

Divorce is not like getting over a cold. This is the amputation of your other half, combined with open-heart surgery, and there's no surgeon at hand to install a new valve, no anaesthetic to numb the pain and no nurses on standby 24 hours a day to attend to your every need. In fact, your heart must learn how to heal itself. As your Divorce Doctor I am here to help, but whether you choose divorce or the choice is made for you, the truth is it's up to you to be as fully prepared as possible for what lies before you.

Being prepared also means attending to the practicalities of everyday living, even when you can't even see straight ahead of you. There are still the bills to pay, the kids to look after, the work to be done, the family to cope with, the lawyers to speak to, and the real pain in your rear end – your soon-to-be ex – to deal with. These are just a few of the dynamics of divorce you'll have to face. Most of all, you need to learn how to look after *yourself* so that you have the energy to look after everything else in your life during your divorce.

It has taken me 14 years to research this book. Coincidentally, that's the same amount of time that I have been divorced. In that time I have studied how people operate in relationships. I've coached hundreds of individuals and couples, some of whom you'll hear from in this book, and many of whom you'll identify with. (I have changed their names and some identifying details to ensure their privacy). What I have discovered is that relationship breakdown transcends religion or race. Surviving divorce and healing your heart are one of the biggest challenges you'll ever face regardless of your cultural or political beliefs.

This too will pass. It's a simple fact of being human that as time passes you are more able to remove yourself from the intensity of any painful experience. Like every other phase in your life, you will not hold on for ever to the fervent feelings you have right now – unless you truly want to. And then, honestly, you can hold on to them, embellish them and be in the drama called 'divorce' for as long as you want. I can only offer you an alternative prescription. Using it is up to you. However, if your other choice is upset and anger, what have you got to lose?

How This Book Works

Each chapter begins with the Three As: Awareness of your situation, Attitude – how you choose to deal with it, and Action – because nothing happens without action.

Each chapter explores a different aspect of divorce and ends with a specific prescription and some 'affirmation medicine' with instructions for use.

Each prescription is designed to facilitate your healing through your personal understanding of your emotions and reactions at each stage of this disease. Each prescription will make you think hard during its prescribed course. Ultimately each prescription has been created to put you in control of your healing process. The more vigilant you are in taking the full course prescribed, the easier and less painful your recovery will be.

Know that your emotions are unpredictable. They will oscillate back and forth depending on the day's events. It could be that the sun is shining and your spirits are lifted. A few minutes later a tactless comment from a well-meaning friend sends you spiralling downwards. You may believe that you have your anger licked and, suddenly, for no apparent reason, there it is raising its ugly head once again.

When this happens – and it will – revisit the relevant section once again, repeat the prescription and know that this is *perfectly normal*.

There will be times, possibly right now, when you feel like you are walking around in a haze or trying to wade through porridge. In the first place, I am going to help you learn to cope on a daily basis.

You may find some of what I have prescribed hard to swallow and very challenging. Like using any new muscle, it will take some time for you to build up your strength in certain areas. Some prescriptions may be easier to fill. Stick with it all. These are tried-and-tested treatments which will work if you use them. Be patient. This has been incubating for a while now, so it won't go away overnight.

There may be some extra medication needed along the way. Perhaps some injections of faith and courage, the odd X-ray to see what's going on below the surface. You may need to make some changes in your nutrition and fitness plans, and you will certainly need to take time to examine your own personal emotional growth. This is a tough time for you; however, it really is true that tough times never last, but tough people do.

At the end of the book there's further support, should you want it, with regular check-ups to keep you well and healthy. If you are truly committed to getting over divorce and going forward with your life, then I look forward to being your Divorce Doctor and helping you heal.

So what are we waiting for? Let's get you on the path to full recovery.

First Things First

From the early stages and for the foreseeable future (especially if you have children), how you react to your ex-partner at any given time will determine whether your experience of divorce will be painful or peaceful. Later on we'll examine in detail what happened, why it happened and the roles both of you played in your relationship's demise. Right now, however, you need emergency treatment to help you deal immediately with everyday issues that can easily escalate into unnecessary suffering.

In the days and weeks to come, you can expect that you and your ex-partner will experience a great deal of hurt and upset. There will be angry confrontations, below-the-belt threats, finding ways of making life as difficult as possible for each other and arguments about just about anything and everything. Perhaps this already sounds familiar?

The 'Something' that Happens

There is a predictable pattern that you'll begin to notice ... 'Something' happens.

There is always a 'something' that happens, even if it's simply a frightening thought about what could occur that would have a negative impact on one of you. Maybe you receive a bill you were not expecting, perhaps your ex is making it difficult for you to see the kids; it may be that finances are extremely tight or it could be that having to continue to live under the same roof is becoming intolerable. Because you are being hit where it hurts and your choices are limited, your immediate reaction is to fight back, resist the reality of the situation, or withdraw completely. Predictably, your partner will react to your reactions by fighting back, resisting or withdrawing, and the cycle goes on.

Lisa has long black hair and stunning legs. She looks like Roxie Hart from *Chicago*. She is a colour therapist. She is gentle and creative. She met Tony at a spiritual awareness seminar. He is Italian and almost too good-looking. He manufactures shirts. His best friend took him to the seminar after insisting that 'making friends with the universe is vital in order to expand your business'. He is sceptical but ambitious. He is willing, he thinks, to let the universe into his business – as a silent partner.

Lisa and Tony are two beautiful people; the attraction is instant. They fall in lust and from the beginning their relationship is volatile. He is jealous and suspicious of her friends. She is flattered by his possessiveness – until it becomes smothering. She is constantly defending and justifying her actions to him. She can't breathe. They break up and then get back together again. After two years it's obvious that living apart is even harder than living together, so they decide to marry. Lisa believes that Tony will finally feel safe. She has chosen him above all others. In the back of her mind she has a niggling feeling that this isn't really the answer, but she quickly brushes it aside and is caught up with the magic of their glamorous wedding. Most of the time she loves being loved by him. However, instead of calming down, marriage means that Tony turns up the volume on his insecurities. He becomes controlling and demanding.

The marriage lasts five years and they have one child, Louis, now three years old. Lisa cannot cope any more. She puts on two stone. Subconsciously she wants Tony to let her go. He won't do that while she is beautiful. She gets fat. He hates her for it and has an affair with a young buyer. This is her get-out-of-jail card. But it doesn't come for free. The marriage ends with resentment and animosity. Tony makes life difficult for Lisa. Forgets to pay bills. The phone is cut off. The nursery fees are due and he tells her she will have to get a 'proper job' and pull her weight. He says that now she is two stone heavier, she has plenty of weight to pull. She tells her lawyer that he is being abusive to her and is refusing to pay for his son. The lawyer writes another letter and asks Lisa for more money on deposit. Lisa tells Tony that he cannot see his son unless he pays up. The battle begins in earnest.

The Cycle of Conflict

From the outset, I want you to know that, in my experience over the years, this pattern is inevitable with 90 per cent of couples in conflict. The only result of this cycle, though, is that barriers are put up, connection is completely lost, the ability to solve the problem or resolve the issue is unlikely and, because you feel so right and justified about your position, serious damage is done when it could have been avoided.

Reaction Management

You have two choices. You can either react in a way that fuels the fire and probably has a detrimental impact on both of you, or you can simply **stop playing the 'blame game'**. It only takes one person to decide not to react for the whole game to fall apart. Easy to say, but harder to do without the right tools. I have designed the following strategies to give you immediate pain relief when conflict rears its head. They are tried and tested and they work. All you have to do is use them.

Taking Your Emotional Temperature

The early stages of relationship breakdown are volatile and unpredictable. Normal life is put on hold and uncertainty is the only certainty you have. You are bound to feel vulnerable and possibly out of control. This is a crazy time. So, before you make any rash decisions or say something you may very well regret shortly after it has left your mouth, I want you to be prepared.

The first thing you need to do is to find out how you are feeling at any given time.

Your Emotional Temperature

Your emotional temperature dictates your mood and how you behave as a consequence. Checking your emotional temperature will give you a greater awareness of how you are feeling in the present moment. This gives you the opportunity to question what has raised or lowered the temperature. Armed with more clarity, you are now better placed to choose your reaction to what's happening rather than operating on automatic reflex. It's the automatic reflex that will most likely lead to even more upset and raise the temperature even higher.

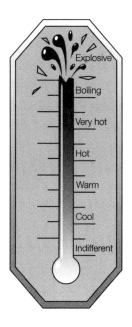

Your Emotional Temperature Gauge

The temperature levels are gauged from indifferent to explosive. I want you to check your temperature by asking yourself the following questions:

1. What is my main/overriding feeling at this time? (Hurt, afraid, sad, lonely?)
2. What is my emotional temperature right now? (Where would you tick the gauge on the side of the thermometer?)
3. Where is my emotional temperature generally on this specific issue? The importance of this issue will impact your temperature. (Where would you tick the gauge on the side of the thermometer?)

Taking Back Control

I know this is may be hard to believe, but you do actually have a *choice* of responses. Right in the moment you may choose to react in a way that gives you immediate pain relief. You may hit back where you can hurt the other person the most, using whatever 'tools' you have available. This may be effective (and, let's face it, even satisfying) in the very short term, but you know in reality that it won't provide sustainable long-term relief.

For now, however, all I want you to do is become aware of your emotional temperature whenever *something happens* that causes you to have an emotional reaction. To help you do this, you need to ask yourself two more questions:

1. What do I believe is causing this temperature level?
2. How will I choose to react?

Your Personal Alarm System

Our bodies are incredibly clever. Every person is different but everyone experiences an emotional reaction in a specific area of their body. For example, when I hear 'something' that makes me want to react, I *feel* it in my chest. I experience a tightening and breathlessness that lets me know that I have a problem with what's being said or done. Some people I have worked with get their 'emotional hit' in their stomachs, others in their shoulders and neck, and others in their heads. Your job is to figure out where you experience your 'emotional hit', because at that very moment your emotional temperature will rise. This feeling is your 'personal alarm system'.

Listening to Your Personal Alarm System

It may be that your ex-partner calls to say that she will be late to pick up the children. You become anxious that you won't be able to get to your appointment on time and angry that she is not keeping her word. Her words 'hit' you straight in your stomach. It's that same old churning feeling you got every time she let you down in the past when you were a couple. Your emotional temperature rises and the conversation you have in your head goes something like this. 'She never considers me; it's always on her terms; this is typical of her,' etc., etc. As a result, by the time she arrives you are at boiling point. It's so easy in this place to let rip and spew out accusations that have stacked-up pain and hurt from the past behind them. However, when you are familiar with your personal alarm system you can do things differently.

- Feel the 'hit' – your personal alarm system
- Observe your emotional temperature rising
- Ask yourself the five questions

Now you need to choose the response that gives you the greatest benefit. So let me explain how you can do that.

Feeling Better Faster

When you have gauged your own emotional temperature, there are specific ways of responding that do not, in turn, raise your ex-partner's emotional temperature. Whatever the situation or the circumstance, your intention is always to create solutions that make *you* feel better as quickly as possible. In order to do this, you have to understand your ex's needs PDQ – pretty damn quick!

When a situation comes up that gives you *your* 'hit' because it looks or sounds like it will have a negative impact on you, it will always be because the other person is coming from their own needs. Perhaps they say something like 'I want the children every Wednesday night' or 'I'm not paying for *that*.' Your job is to understand their needs before launching into defensiveness. You'll hear me say several times throughout this book – '*Every behaviour has a positive intention for the person who is manifesting the behaviour.*'

This means that any request your ex-partner makes, or anything they disagree with or deny you, is because they believe their own needs will not or may not be met if they don't get the answer they want. When you immediately react defensively to their words, you don't give yourself a chance to find out what those needs are. It could be that once you understand their needs, you may be more amenable to them.

For example, one reason your partner may want to see the children on a Wednesday night is because that's the night he/she gets home from work early enough to eat with the children/bath them/do homework with them/take them to an after-school activity. If your partner says 'I'm not paying for *that*,' it may be that they are overwhelmed by the expense and really fearful that they won't be able to cover spiralling costs. It does not necessarily mean that *you* should be paying for '*that*'.

Instead of hearing your partner 'demanding' or trying to 'control' you, it's important that you ask good-quality questions that will help you to understand why they are saying what they have said. You may find this hard to believe, but in the majority of cases it won't be because they specifically want to make *your* life difficult. It's because they want to make *their own* life easier or happier in some way. That's not the same thing at all. Don't get misled by the position they are taking. I have found that it's never the 'presenting' issue that the person is upset or frustrated by. It's always something else that they believe they will lose out on if they don't get their way.

To find out what's going on with the other person, ask good-quality questions. Say something like:

- What are you concerned about?
- What about this is important to you?
- What would that give you?
- What's wrong with my suggestion?
- What could I do to make my suggestion acceptable to you?
- What's the real problem?
- What about if I/we …?

When you are able to lower your emotional temperature to normal, it's much easier to listen to their response, so that you can calmly explain how you feel and what you need.

Lowering Your Emotional Temperature

One tactic that works in lowering your emotional temperature is to imagine that you are on 'delayed reaction'. You know how when you call a foreign country on the phone, there is often a delay in transmitting your words? Get into the habit of creating a moment's delay before you react. Take a breath, feel the 'hit' and see your emotional temperature in your mind's eye. You'll know instantly where you are. Now switch into your questions, keep breathing and let your emotional temperature ease down with every breath you take.

I'm not asking you to give in to their demands, and you don't have to agree with them. You are not being nice, you are being strategic. Obviously you won't agree to anything that compromises your needs, and neither will they. However, once their needs are out in the open, it gives you the opportunity to understand their position instead of thinking the whole thing is a plot against you. You can then resolve any conflict and reach a solution that works for both of you.

Building Your Mental Muscles

All of the above ideas are designed to build your mental strength. They are *not* about giving your power away. Imagine a boxing ring. Both the boxers facing each other are equally skilled, and it's evens on who will win the match. However, in the ring something happens. Boxer A throws the first punch and takes the lead. Boxer B is taken by surprise at the force of the punch and falls down. Immediately the power shifts to Boxer A; Boxer B is now on the defensive. In an instant the roles are defined and Boxer A becomes mentally more confident that he will win the match. Unless Boxer B can equalize, despite the fact that the two boxers are evenly matched, Boxer A's 'mental muscles' will give him more physical strength and he has every chance of winning the match.

Rebuilding Equality

Whilst this isn't about either of you winning at the expense of the other losing, unless you can equalize your position you will be floored. Equalizing outside the ring will take more brains than brawn. This is about behaving smarter, not working harder. In relationship conflicts this means writing new rules of engagement as a result of understanding your emotional reaction, and making different choices on how to respond. One of the ways to do this is to avoid blame.

How Not to Play the Blame Game

Taking responsibility for your role in any conflict that may arise at this challenging time is probably the last thing you want to do right now. It's so much easier to be right about how wrong the other person is. Let's face it, though, we are not angels. None of us is right 100 per cent of the time. This is not about who is right or wrong. Playing the blame game does not resolve conflict. It only allows the conflict to continue. Resolving conflict is about learning what works and what doesn't, and then taking the necessary actions to move forward.

Recognizing your role in the relationship breakdown is something we will go into in more detail later, but right now, however resistant you are to the idea of negotiating current conflicts with your ex-partner, my experience shows that the alternative usually turns out to be painful, messy and very expensive.

Past Conflicts

Let's look at how you behaved in the past when you were in conflict.

Think about a past conflict, either with your partner, a family member, a work colleague or a friend. Ask yourself:

- What did I do that contributed to that conflict?
- How could I have handled the situation better?
- Have I suffered because of my own actions?
- Have others suffered because of my actions?

Come back to the present and ask yourself:

- What is the most important lesson I learned from that conflict?

Now, armed with your answers, think about a current conflict. Ask yourself:

- Right now, how would my life improve if this conflict were resolved?
- What would I have to do in order to let go of this current conflict completely?
- What would happen if I did let go of it completely?

It's impossible to control other people. It's even more impossible to control your ex-partner with all the heightened emotions that are in the mix. You can only control yourself.

The great thing about that is it means you *can* control how *you* cope with your ex-partner and others with whom you are in conflict.

'Be the Change You Want to See in the World'

Ghandi knew that people would not believe in him or support him unless he showed them how committed he was to making changes. *He* had to be the change that he wanted to see in the world. Nelson Mandela and Mother Teresa did likewise. Now, I know that they didn't have your ex to deal with, and nothing could be anywhere near as challenging as that! But don't hold your breath expecting your ex to change first. You need to change yourself and how you choose to react at any given time. You need to realize that you have all the power you need to be able to do that. It only takes one person to lower the temperature – and that's you. By lowering your emotional temperature and intentionally seeking resolution, you hold the key to changing your relationship with your ex-partner and how you deal with the inevitable disagreements that will arise. When you change your own behaviour, you also change the reaction that you get from your ex-spouse, and that's the first step to learning to deal with conflict differently.

Your Personal Prescription: Directions for Use

You are required to put yourself under observation.

Your job is to get into the habit of consistently gauging your emotional temperature every time you experience an 'emotional hit' in your body. This is about choosing your attitude and deciding how to react in any situation.

At this early stage of your treatment, I want to raise your awareness and help you become fully conscious so that you to begin to discover for yourself what might stand in the way of your healing. I want to help you understand the behaviours that will best serve you as you start the road to recovery.

Dosage

When you have answered the questions below, I'd like you to refer back to them twice a day for the next five days. Feel free to make any changes to your answers on a daily basis. Create a journal that will be your Divorce Diary (for more about how useful this can be, see page 52). Keep a note of your emotions and gauge your emotional temperature each time you read through the questions.

- Taking away any blame, what's the reality of my personal situation right now?
- Taking away any blame or guilt, what am I resisting?
- How do I feel when I resist?
- How do I behave as a result?
- How would I prefer to behave?
- How would I benefit from behaving that way?

Self-Affirmation Medicine

The following affirmations must be repeated at least three times each, three times per day, for five consecutive days. Decide what times work best for you. First thing in the morning when you are feeling rested and before you start your day works well; mid-morning is another great time, and after lunch with the afternoon ahead will carry you through to the evening.

I will face my fears courageously today.
Today, I am responsible for my reactions and behaviours.
I am gaining emotional strength every day.

Chapter 2
Intensive Care

Awareness	Of your feelings and what they mean
Attitude	Choosing how you will deal with them
Action	The most effective actions for dealing with your feelings

Breaking Up Is Hard to Do

During her particularly long and acrimonious divorce, my friend Sally had a wonderful response to people who asked her how she was feeling. She would say 'Average to s**t' which, whilst not the most elegant turn of phrase, does rather hit the spot. I have to tell you that what Sally was experiencing, you too will feel at one time or another.

Facing Your Feelings

In the intensive-care stage of your break-up, the full force of your feelings will probably smack you in the face. Even if your relationship was well past its sell-by date, and even if you initiated the break-up, the loss of a long-term relationship is a tangible and painful experience.

The different feelings and their accompanying sensations in your body are not good or bad, right or wrong, they are just feelings. They come and go – it seems for no obvious reason at the time – and they bring with them a whole host of reactions. I don't tell you this because I want you to feel like you are in some kind of purgatory or that you are being punished for some crime you were not even aware of committing. I tell you this because I want you to be aware of what's happening at these early stages so there are no surprises and you know what to expect. Your job is to allow these emotions, understand them, know that they have an important message for you and be willing to find out what that message is.

Snakes and Ladders (and Other Conundrums)
Alice and the Caterpillar

> **Caterpillar:** *Who are YOU?*
>
> *(This was not an encouraging opening for a conversation.)*
>
> *Alice:* I -- I hardly know, sir, just at present -- at least,
> I know who I was when I got up this morning, but I think I
> must have been changed several times since then.

Alice may have been in Wonderland, but you are in 'I wonder' land. No one wants to be here. It's a country full of indecision and unpredictable feelings. In this land, all the inhabitants wonder how they will travel the rocky terrain laid out before them. It's a changeable place where nothing stays the same for very long and uncertainty is the only thing you can be sure of. In this chapter my aim is to help you leave this inhospitable land as quickly as possible. To do this you need skills and strategies borrowed from various therapies to help you navigate your route to the border.

What Exactly Will I Feel?
Most people in 'I wonder' land will experience a variety of emotions during the course of one 12-hour day. It would be so much easier if we didn't have these damn feelings to deal with, but they come with

the territory. Fear and panic, sadness and grief, blame and anger are interrupted by moments of hope and faith, friendship and love. Within minutes you can easily slide back down to guilt, rejection and numbness again. It's no surprise to hear people tell me that they just can't think straight. This is a game of emotional snakes and ladders: two steps forward, two steps back, and so on. I have illustrated this process for you in the form of a board game (see overleaf) because for the next weeks (and probably months) ahead you can expect your emotions and feelings to be as unpredictable as the role of a dice.

Manage Your Thoughts and You Can Manage Your Emotions

Having the mental strength and physical stamina to make it out of 'I wonder' land as speedily as possible will depend on how you manage yourself on a daily basis. And how you do that will be dictated almost entirely by how you manage your emotions.

Here's How It Works

- Your thoughts impact your emotions.
- Your emotions define your attitude to your life, which in turn dictates your behaviour.
- Your behaviour will dictate the response you get from other people, and that response dictates how you react emotionally.

All of which takes us back to the fact that your recovery process and leaving your own personal 'I wonder' land is dictated almost entirely by how you manage your thoughts.

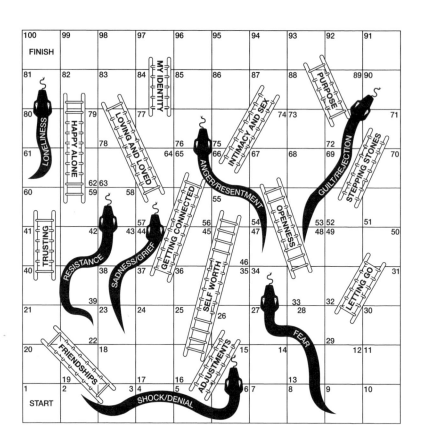

How We Create Our Own Pain

Pain is the result of a story we tell ourselves about the way 'it' is. For example, most people will agree that when you go through separation and divorce, some of your losses may include:

- the family home
- mutual friends
- access to the children
- family life

- money
- hopes for the future
- intimacy
- personal pride and status
- companionship.

This is by no means a comprehensive list and I am sure you could add some other losses that are specific to you. Both of us could find examples of people who have experienced a great deal of pain as a result of these losses. Certainly, at the time of my divorce I would say that I was one of them. But there is something I have discovered over the years through my studies, through my clients and through my own personal experience:

Emotional pain only exists when you put a specific meaning on it.

Your 'Story' of What Pain Means

Look at the above list. Let's take access to the children. Many fathers will tell you that being apart from their children on a daily basis, even if they have regular contact with them, is very painful. That's completely understandable, and the truth is that anyone who loves their kids will physically miss being away from them on a daily basis. But it's the 'story' of what someone makes being apart from their children *mean* that engenders even more pain. Their thoughts run wild as they make up all kinds of scenarios in their minds which, if they happened, would cause the utmost pain.

Perhaps a father thinks it means that they could be forgotten by their children, that some other person might take their place or that they won't be loved as much because they are not there. This may happen and it may not. Many of us would say that no matter how our parents behave, even if they are abusive, there remains a part of us that still loves them and longs for them to love us in the way we'd like to be loved. If you have been the kind of father who goes to work, comes home, spends time with your kids and is (as much as anyone is) normal, your kids will not forget you and will continue to love you.

However, when we write the story in our minds that our children will forget us, the pain is almost unbearable. Our thoughts fool us into thinking that we will be forced out by a surrogate parent and that not seeing our children on a daily basis will mean the end of our close relationship. We imagine that our partners will leave the country and take the kids with them and we will never see them again. We cause ourselves so much pain (even though these things have not happened and may never happen) that we can become physically and mentally ill.

I'm not saying that the pain is not real when you feel it. What I'm saying is that how you feel at any given time is in direct response to the *meaning* you are putting on what is happening to you, to others or to the world around you.

Holding on to your beliefs about how the circumstances of your life will impact you negatively keeps you firmly in your story of 'what it means', which is not always the truth.

Thought Stopping

There is only one thing more powerful than our thoughts, and that is our breath.

Many meditation techniques concentrate on the breath, and most relaxation techniques involve focusing on your breathing. This is because when you are concentrating on your breathing it is pretty difficult to hold any other thoughts in your head. Try it right now and you will see what I mean.

> Put your hand on your stomach and take a deep breath in until your stomach fills up like a big balloon.
> Hold the breath for as long as you can and then exhale through your mouth. Do this three times.

While you were taking those deep breaths, I'm pretty sure you were unable to hold any other thoughts in your mind. That's how you know that your breath is more powerful than your thoughts.

Some people can get a head rush doing this because it's not usual for us to breathe into our diaphragms like this all the time. Most of us breathe very shallowly, taking short little breaths in and out. This kind of breathing is guaranteed to keep us in an alert state most of the time, but it isn't effective when you want to change your mental and physical state from anxious to calm.

Knowing this means that you have a very powerful tool at your disposal. In order to stop your thoughts racing around and making up all kinds of scenarios that scare the pants off you, take a deep breath into your diaphragm, hold it, exhale through your mouth and repeat – around five times. Your mind will become clearer and your emotional temperature will decrease so that you have the mental ability to *respond* constructively instead of *reacting* out of fear or panic.

Now that you are a little more calm, the next part of the exercise is to change your thoughts. To do this you need to have some new thoughts available that have absolutely nothing to do with the upsetting thoughts that got you into this state in the first place.

To create a stock of these thoughts, recall five scenarios where you were incredibly relaxed, happy, laughing and enjoying what was going on around you. I return to my special rock in Mallorca and can place myself on its edge watching the waves hit the rocks below, the water shimmering and the warmth of the sun on my body. Where is your special place? What about a time when you were really having fun? Perhaps you were dancing, scuba diving, driving your new car, walking through beautiful countryside. Prepare five wonderful memories of good times and special places and write them down in your Divorce Diary.

For the next month, keep a large elastic band comfortably on your wrist. When something happens to upset you, shout 'STOP!' (out loud if you are on your own, or in your head if you happen to be in the supermarket or any other public place) and snap the band on your wrist. The shock of the snap on your wrist will serve to change your mental and physical state. (If you happen to be driving your car, pull over as soon as you can.) Now start your breathing technique (no one will notice, I promise), taking five deep breaths into your diaphragm, holding it as long as you can and exhaling slowly through your mouth. Now recall one of your scenarios and really experience it in your mind. Remember where you were, see what you were seeing, feel what you were feeling and hear the sounds around you.

If you have been very upset, you may wish to recall another of your lovely scenarios in order to restabilize yourself. Once again, really experience it in your mind. Remember where you were, see what you were seeing, feel what you were feeling and hear the sounds around you.

Do this as many times as necessary in order to restabilize yourself mentally and physically. When you are ready to return to the present you will have put some distance between what you were originally thinking and how you now feel, and you will be much calmer and more able to think of a suitable solution to the immediate problem.

It's a simple technique and one that has been tried and tested and works really well. It's very difficult for us to stop our minds from having upsetting thoughts. They arrive from nowhere and we can go from feeling pretty much OK one minute to feeling awful the next. Don't waste time trying to work out why; just use the technique to change your state, come back to the present and take whatever actions are necessary to continue with your day.

Will I Feel Everything?

Recently I went on a special diet. Each day was planned with specific meals containing all the foods I could eat. There was far more than I was used to eating. So I looked at the list of 'helpful questions and answers' and discovered that I did not have to eat everything on the list each day. The same theory applies to the feelings you might experience during this period of intensive care. You don't have to experience *all* of them in order to heal.

Some people manage to bypass particular feelings because they simply don't apply to their specific circumstances. So the ones I talk about here are set out as examples and to assure you that, if you do experience them, it's perfectly normal and you are not going mad.

The Stages of Divorce

Many therapists and authors have attempted to categorize the stages of loss, and many have likened it to a bereavement. I have chosen to use Dr Elisabeth Kübler-Ross's 'stages of grief' as a guide to what many people go through on their journey to recovery:

Denial	*This can't be happening to me. I don't believe it.*
Anger	*Why me? It's not fair. NO! NO! NO! How dare you?*
Bargaining	*Let's wait till the children leave home. I'll do anything.*
Depression	*I'm so sad. I feel so guilty. What's the point? I'm going to die.*
Acceptance	*I'm letting go. I can handle it. I'm moving forward with my life.*

There is no specific order for these main phases, that's why it's a game of snakes and ladders. It's illogical, but emotions are not logical. So you will fluctuate back and forth. However, mostly everyone will finally reach a place of acceptance when, having gone through the whole emotional process, it becomes unarguably clear that there is no longer any point investing time and energy into a relationship that has nothing to give in return. We will explore these stages in more detail in this chapter – with the exception of Acceptance, which we will look at in more detail in Chapter 8.

What Is Grief?

The most common symptoms of the grieving process are crying, sighing, hallucinating, weight change, lack of concentration, change in sleeping patterns, excessive eating/drinking/smoking and depression. For sure you will recognize some of these symptoms in yourself. You have moved from organization to disorganization. You are in a state of flux. The goal of grief – and yes, there is a goal to grief – is to get you to a place where you can reorganize your life once again.

So what might be standing in your way?

My Story

My inability to grieve certainly stood in my way and made the process of my divorce so much harder than it needed to be. I was far too impatient to wallow around in my pain. My marriage was over and I just wanted to wipe the slate clean as quickly as possible.

The shock I experienced when my marriage ended left me with an odd numbness that made it harder for me to feel anything. As I am impatient, this numbness was great for me because it meant I could just get on with my life. I didn't even have to think. I couldn't. I switched into survival mode and became resilient and pragmatic. I was rather proud that I had such inner strength. I was able to get into action, get on with my life and become a 'human doing'.

The downside is that I put becoming a feeling 'human being' on hold. Yes, I visited a counsellor, but I didn't' 'need' it. In fact, I reasoned, it was only because my counselling exams required me to do so. However, I remember one specific day when my confidence and belief in myself were still in the construction phase and I had been unwell. I was feeling somewhat fragile and, during the counselling session, we got to the place where the tears started to flow. It was scary and I was furious with myself. I put an end to our sessions there and then and never went back. I had two small children, very little money and no time for tears. I simply couldn't allow myself to become vulnerable in case I fell apart. I zipped up my suit of protective armour, bought every self-help book available, repaired my make-up and carried on.

What I didn't understand was that every time you lose something, especially something as life-changing as a 15-year marriage, there is a need to grieve. The goal of the grieving process and all that it contains is to give you time to reflect on your old life and redesign your new life the way you want it to be. Grieving gives you the opportunity to get your feelings out into the open and examine the cues and clues they give you about what's really going on in your life.

One day, probably into the second year of operating my life on automatic pilot, I was invited to a women's group set up so that women could listen to each other and talk openly about anything and everything. I was sceptical; it was all a bit 'Laura Ashley' for me. I like to think that I'm far more 'Versace'. For some reason, though, I went and I was shocked at what happened. I felt something inside me seize up. I felt a pain so intense and numbing that I was virtually frozen to my chair. I didn't speak during the entire group, I just cried the whole time. I was safe amongst them, no one had to ask me how

I was feeling, no one felt the need to make me a cup of tea; they just let me cry. And I began to 'feel'. It was surreal and yet comforting, and all these years later I can still feel the warmth of the group and think of it gratefully as a catalyst that heralded the beginning of my own healing process.

What Are You Afraid Of?

Some of my grief contained the following fears: 'I won't be able to manage on my own,' 'I don't earn enough money,' 'I won't have enough time for my children if I have to work full time,' 'I'm not clever enough to get a good job,' 'I'll never be loved again,' 'I'll never be able to do the things I wanted to do,' 'I'm a failure,' 'I'll never find anyone to take care of me and make me laugh so much,' etc.

With fears like these I could stay frozen in panic for days. Was that helpful? Of course not! If this is where you are right now, you probably know you are being your own worst enemy.

My definition of fear is:

Future
Expectations
Appearing
Real.

Most of what we are afraid of never happens. It's far more painful *imagining* what may happen. That's why my acronym puts fear as a phenomenon that lives in the future. Because human beings are so evolved we can actually feel the pain of something that hasn't even happened yet. In order to build your courage and emotional resilience, you need to live in the present and face your fears head on.

Armed with this knowledge, let's look at the first stage of grief.

Shock and Denial

Roy Taylor comes to see me, ashen-faced, with a sad tale to tell. A veteran of many London-to-Brighton runs and a classic car collector, he's a tall, well-built man with gentle brown eyes and a rugged complexion. He has been happily married for 39 years to Wendy, the mother of his three grown daughters. Life has been prosperous but not without its challenges along the way. During his long career, Roy, an engineer, has travelled around the world for his company about five times a year for several weeks at a time. Wendy was a traditional wife and mother and she looked after the home and children whilst Roy was away. A slight woman with mousy hair and an English rose complexion, she had never really lived up to her own potential. She was a reporter on the local newspaper when she'd met Roy. She was covering the London-to-Brighton run when she interviewed him at the finish line. She had secretly harboured dreams of working for a big national newspaper. However, her dreams stayed safely in harbour when she gave up work to marry Roy. There was no need for her small salary, and falling pregnant as quickly as she did meant that motherhood took over as her main occupation. So she progressed naturally into the life of a Surrey housewife.

As her family grew and Roy's career took off, Wendy was able to have help in the house and she always maintained a good circle of friends. Yet sometimes on Roy's return from another business trip abroad, Wendy would be less than welcoming. She was prone to periods of melancholy where she would withdraw into herself for several days. Unfortunately for Roy, these lapses always seemed to coincide with his return from business trips. He would be disappointed, of course, but he reasoned that perhaps she'd been lonely and had found it hard to cope without him.

On several occasions he tried to find out what was wrong but Wendy could offer no reason; she said she didn't know why. After a few days she'd come back to her old self, so Roy learned not to pressurize her when she was like this and instead rationalized that perhaps it was just a transition she had to make between him leaving and coming back home.

The years passed, the children left home and Roy retired but kept a part-time position as a troubleshooter for the company. He travelled much less frequently, maybe twice a year, and Wendy's withdrawals lessened. However, one day he arrived home from a short trip to Jersey to find a note. It said, 'I'm leaving you. I've had enough, Wendy.'

There was no explanation, nothing had happened in the previous weeks or months that had led Roy to believe that Wendy was upset about anything in particular. Everything had seemed perfectly normal to him. Wendy had walked and he just hadn't seen it coming.

For the entire first session with me, Roy cried. Great heaving sobs racked his body. He struggled to breathe and the only comfort that I could give him was to be there with him. The shock of Wendy's leaving was a tsunami that flooded his body and mind with great waves of pain. He was incapable of speech. When he eventually came up for air he choked out that he just couldn't believe it, couldn't understand it or make sense of it and didn't know what he had done to cause it. Where was she? What was her state of mind? He was worried about her welfare as well as being engulfed by his own pain. He tried to convince himself that she would come back. He moved into denial. If he didn't pressure her, he was sure she would return to 'normal' just like she had done in the past.

He stayed close to the phone but it didn't ring. After several weeks, he heard via his eldest daughter that Wendy was safe. Wendy had rented a Regency bay-fronted apartment on the seafront in Brighton. She had grown up there, and it had always been a place of refuge for her. Of all the wonderful places they had visited around the world together, Brighton was 'home'. Roy questioned his daughter but she refused to discuss Wendy. She simply said, 'Mum needs space.' To Roy, it felt like a conspiracy. His youngest daughter urged Roy to accept that Mum might not come back. His middle girl said she didn't want to interfere but that 'Mum is doing OK.'

For almost a year, Roy lives in 'I wonder' land and cannot move forward. He doesn't know if his marriage is over, he doesn't know if there is a chance to rebuild it, all he knows is that he wants Wendy back and he wants his life back. It's the not knowing, the wondering, that makes the pain so unbearable. He writes Wendy a letter asking her to just please explain what has happened. He promises not to pursue her. He just wants to understand. There is no reply. He writes again. He carries on hoping that she will come back. She doesn't.

Roy realizes that there is absolutely nothing he can do. In between his tears we begin our work.

Compounded Pain

In Roy's case the length of his relationship compounded the pain of loss. If you have spent half a lifetime together, it's hard to recall what life was like before your partner. Roy had been invested emotionally, physically and financially with Wendy for 39 years. On a spiritual level, he truly believed that his soul had mated with Wendy's. He thought that they were two halves of a whole.

There are many different kinds of pain. The pain of being rejected, the pain of confusion and disorientation, the pain of denial – and the pain for Roy of the really big unanswered question: why did my marriage fall apart?

The Power of Pain

Pain is frightening because when we feel it we cannot imagine how we will overcome it or, even if we do overcome it, what will become of us. But pain is a wake-up call. It has a purpose. It's a precursor to change. For many of us, it's not until we are in deep pain that we can take an honest look at our lives and ask ourselves some seriously deep questions about who we are, how we have operated in our lives and what we really want.

In the beginning the only thing that Roy wanted was Wendy. Only Wendy would be able to relieve the intensity of his emotional freefall into the unknown. But pain has a purpose, even for Roy. Without fully experiencing his pain, I knew that Roy would not move up the ladder of recovery. There was a deeper learning for Roy, but until he was able to control his pain, we would not be able to dig deeper. I offered him the following strategies to help him be present with his pain and learn how to manage it so it didn't overwhelm him.

What's the Purpose of Pain?

Pain is nature's way of helping us acknowledge our hurt. It's natural and healthy and to be expected. As I said, it's completely normal to feel a whole range of emotions on the road to your recovery. In fact, it's necessary for you to *feel* in order to *heal*. The numbness I felt right at the beginning of my own divorce journey meant that I was still in shock. Numbness and shock are the precursors to the rest of the feeling experience.

In that weird world called 'this can't be happening to me', you go round and round in your mind trying to make sense of your situation. It's like a helter-skelter ride: hour by hour, day by day, the climb continues and finally you reach the pinnacle. You are dizzy with emotion. In order to get grounded again, you'll have to grab your mat and hold on tight if you want to come back down to earth in an upright position.

Learning to Live with Your Pain

Pain has a life of its own. Literally. Think of pain as an entity that you will be in relationship with for the near future. Pain lives and breathes and accompanies you during your daily life for a period of time. It's here for a purpose and when it has done its job, it leaves – but only pain can decide when that time is.

To release pain sooner rather than later, you must allow it to run its natural course. It demands to be experienced and not resisted. By resisting pain you are resisting reality. The reality is that you are hurting. Trying to stuff it down or put on a brave face – 'big boys (and girls) don't cry' is futile. The pain remains. What we resist persists.

Your job is to move in with your pain and let it take up residence within you.

Crying to Release Pain

Allowing your pain to be with you and actually embracing it as part of your healing process is extremely beneficial. I can promise that you will grow and learn from experiencing your feelings. I can also say that I have found that the men and women who deny their feelings deny their own personal growth. And, by the way, a word about tears. Crying releases the stress and toxins that pain produces.

Unfortunately, not everyone can cry. Some people bottle it all up or express it through other behaviours. These are often confusing for other people because no one can feel or see your pain, so if you cannot express it in language, you could inadvertently destroy other important relationships in your life by behaving in ways that can be misconstrued.

However, Roy was not one to stuff down his feelings. He was excellent at crying and I was pleased that he had this capacity. My method for helping him 'let his pain in' instead of resisting it is simple.

Surfing the Pain

Just for a moment, play back a video in your mind's eye of the images you have seen of surfers tackling the big waves. My personal memories take me to Cornwall where the winds attract tanned wet-suited free spirits who travel the coastline in camper vans looking for the best waves. I've seen them out there on blustery days and marvelled at how they can stay on the boards. Even if you have only seen them on TV, you'll know what I'm talking about.

Now recall what they do when a huge wave comes towards them. Do they turn their boards to face the wave head on? Not likely. If they did they would be engulfed by it and probably

---

swallow a great deal of water. What they do is turn their boards towards the beach, so that they 'catch' the wave and surf into the shore on its crest. Then, when they reach the safety of the shallows, they pick up their boards and either return out to sea or sit on the sand and watch the other surfers do their thing.

Surfing the waves of pain copies the principles of surfing for real. Here's how it works:

- Something happens. (Remember, there's always a 'something' that happens.) It could be a thought, a memory or something as innocent as noticing your ex's favourite magazine on sale when you stop off to buy the paper. It triggers an emotional reaction in you and you begin to feel the first waves of pain.
- If you can, find a quiet safe place to sit or lie down.
- Instead of resisting it, allow the wave of pain to come towards you. Let it in. Welcome it; you know it has a purpose.
- Now imagine you are a surfer. Take your board and do as the surfers do. Turn it so that you can surf the wave of pain.
- Ride the wave of pain in the direction it's going. As soon as you are on the wave it's only ever moving towards its own demise. Allow yourself to cry, shout, hit pillows and go as crazy as you safely can. Get it all out. Turn up the volume. Really feel that pain and let it permeate your body. Don't try and control it, don't judge it or resist it, just let yourself go and feel it with every fibre of your being.
- Then notice what happens. How do you feel after surfing the wave of pain? You are probably drained and need to rest for a

while, but as you calm down and reach the safety of your own shallows, something different will happen to you emotionally and physically.

It's a strange phenomenon, but most people report that their pain begins to subside of its own accord. It instinctively knows when you are done. If you try to control it and end it prematurely, it will know that it's not quite over. You'll have to get back on your board and surf some more. Let your pain dictate its pace to you, not the other way round.

After your pain subsides and you are spent, you'll have time for reflection. Take this quiet time to ask yourself:

- What was the purpose of that wave of pain?
- What is my pain here to teach me?
- Has my pain got other associations? Was I remembering other times in the past when I have been hurt? What were those times about?
- Is the pain telling me about something that I need to give myself rather than have others provide for me? If so, what is it that I need to give myself right now?

Obviously if you are at work, driving the car or carrying out some other everyday task, you will not be able to sit down, lie down or take time out. However, once you have experienced surfing the pain at a time when you do have the luxury of privacy, at the first hint of an approaching wave of pain, if circumstance dictates that you need to hold it back, notice what has triggered it and play it out later in a more appropriate place.

Crossing the Pain Barrier

The more conscious you become when experiencing pain, the easier it becomes to cross your pain barrier and cope with your loss. It doesn't sound like much fun, I know, but trust me; I'm a 'doctor'. Pain is part of a package designed ultimately to help you feel better and take you to a place of understanding about what happened, why it happened and how it happened so you can ultimately move forward with your life.

There's no question that crossing your own personal pain barrier with your sanity intact is challenging, but with the right strategies you will do it, and you will emerge stronger for it.

Yes, this is the part of your journey where it's easy to feel like you are going quite mad. But the 'pain game' must be played to win. The ultimate prize is acceptance. Until you can accept the end of your relationship, you will delay the moment when you are ready to rebuild your life.

Bargaining – the Fear inside the Pain

To get to a place of acceptance you still have a couple more stops along the way. Bargaining is next on the agenda. This is where one or the other of you starts making deals. 'Let's not make hasty decisions, how about you take some time to think and then we'll talk?' 'If I change would you consider …?' 'You can have the kids this weekend if I can take them to my parents for two weeks.' 'You can't see the kids until I get more money.'

All bargaining is based on the fear of unmet needs, which could cause even more pain. In order to understand the fears that lurk beneath the surface of bargaining you'll need to lower your emotional temperature and ask yourself some questions that will help you distinguish the truth from the story. Questions like, 'What is the fear that allows me to bargain with my ex?' 'What might happen if I cannot get my ex to bargain with me?'

The answers you'll receive will allow you to address the specific situation and take actions that may alleviate your fears.

You may be able to persuade yourself that bargaining means you are being fair and adult. You may dress it up as give and take. But if your bargaining hides an underlying fear of some kind, you are simply being dishonest to yourself.

Face your fear. Feel those uncomfortable feelings and then have the courage to make requests without making deals. You may not always get the answer you want, but your honesty will allow your ex to hear what you really want rather than criticism, judgement or manipulation. You will be able to come to a resolution that is far cleaner, clearer and more honest. If you are not able to do this, you will find that the pain may linger much longer than is necessary.

Turning Anger Outside In

Our next stage along the grief journey is anger.

At one point or another you will feel angry. No question about it. Anger has its place and can be good because it means you are no longer in denial and have moved out of numbness into an awareness of what's happening in your life. Anger is an emotion with far more life in it than denial – however, it can be a dangerous emotion if you don't understand where it comes from and how to manage it appropriately. We have all heard stories of partners who 'accidentally' wreck their ex's car, or sabotage some important business meeting or even cause their partners physical harm. Unbridled anger can have severe consequences.

The problem starts because we believe our anger is caused by the other person. It's true that on many occasions their behaviour has *provoked* our anger. However, that's not the full story.

There's a great line in the film *Pretty Woman* when Edward Lewis (Richard Gere) is in the bath with Vivien Ward (Julia Roberts) and they are talking about Edward's father. Edward says it cost him $10,000 worth of therapy to be able to say 'I am angry at my father.' We guess that he must have been in a great deal of pain to spend that kind of money to get his anger articulated.

My belief is that anger is the outward expression of internal pain and, more often than not, a person is far angrier with themselves for allowing an unacceptable behaviour to continue or putting themselves in a situation where they could not get the care and love that they needed for as long as they did. Of course, when we are children we don't have a choice, but as married adults we did and do.

When I hear a client say, 'I am so angry at him or her' for whatever reason, I ask them to look beneath the surface of their anger to find out whether it really is the other person they are angry with. Is it perhaps really themselves? Even if they are resistant at first, they always realize that they are even angrier with themselves for having allowed themselves to be hurt by another person.

At a time where it's much easier to point the finger, I am asking you to look inward and take personal responsibility for your own behaviour. Have you *allowed* the other person to dishonour you in the way they have?

That's a big ask, I know. You'd much rather be right about how wrong they are, and I'll bet you can justify yourself from here till kingdom come and draw up a consensus of opinions in your favour from your whole neighbourhood. Don't waste your time. I mean it. You stuck around for whatever reasons, and they were justifiable reasons at the time, but I'm suggesting that you are now as angry with yourself for doing that as you are with your ex for not being who you wanted them to be.

Here's what I want you to know so you can stop beating yourself (and anyone else around you) up: it's only when you can accept and understand that taking the risk to love someone else and open your heart to them does not always mean they will take care of it or even appreciate it, that you will be able to release your anger at yourself and your partner.

That doesn't mean that you have to keep your heart closed. But it does mean that opening your heart comes with some risks. No one can guarantee that the love you give will be reciprocated for ever. But the alternative is never to open your heart again, and that would be such a waste of all you have to give.

However, *you are responsible for your heart* and whom you give it to, and for finding a way of healing yourself should it get broken again. To direct anger towards your partner for not appreciating the love you gave them is a wasted emotion. It won't get you anywhere and only causes you pain on top of pain.

It's hard to believe right now, but there is a reason this happened to you (which we will look at in the next chapter) and a lesson to learn that will ultimately help you to accept your situation, drop the anger and move towards forgiveness.

Depression

The next stage in the Kübler-Ross process is depression. I believe that most forms of depression are identity issues; I will expand on this theory in more detail later.

Depression is often caused by the thought that everything you believed you were and everything you created around you – that is, the structure of your life – has been taken away from you.

When It All Gets Too Much

For some people the feelings attached to this stage in the grief process are too overwhelming for books like this to help. If you are really panicking and feel like you have virtually disappeared and are becoming invisible to yourself, please heed these warning signals. When life feels pointless and these feelings begin to spiral downwards they can have far-reaching consequences that impact your life and the lives of everyone around you. I can only urge you to get outside help if you feel that you don't want to get up in the morning and are just going through the motions of life.

Some people are emotionally stronger than perhaps they give themselves credit for and are able to navigate their way through by using the kinds of strategies I offer, but you know yourself better than anyone. Take responsibility for yourself and decide if you could benefit from some outside help or not.

If you know that you can keep your head above water and cope on a daily basis, then that's great. But even you may have days when you can't even take pleasure in your children, your work is suffering and you have lost your appetite. You may well experience a sense of failure, hopelessness, loss, despair, fear or overwhelming desperation. Even a short-term relationship holds the fantasy of hopes for the future, so it's heart-wrenching to let go. Many of these feelings are the 'normal' symptoms of the intensive-care part of your recovery. However, on top of this there may be other symptoms that are so unlike your usual demeanour that you realize there is something really wrong. If that's the case, you need to catch it quickly and decide what kind of help you need. I have known people to live in a depressive state for decades without even realizing that they are depressed. Of all the times in your life, this is the one where you most need to look after yourself. I leave it up to your own judgement to decide what's best for you.

Past Hurts

There is another aspect of depression in divorce. When any of us finds ourselves in painful situations, they often remind us of past hurts. This is not something we are necessarily conscious of, but somewhere in the databank of our minds, our brains have associated an upsetting emotion with something that happened way back when. If we do make the connection consciously, sometimes the end of a relationship can remind us of powerful frightening memories of past loss or separation. You may have experienced all kinds of wounds from your past, as far back as your childhood.

Whatever those losses may be for you, ending your love relationship can trigger old associations as past fears resurface. These old associations can compound depression, so it's important to be able to make a distinction between what's happening now and what happened in the past.

Take a look at the following examples. Do any of them resonate with you?

- Have you experienced some form of desertion in the past? You may have lost a loved one early in your life, perhaps one parent was absent or alcoholic, or perhaps you were left somewhere for a long time when you were supposed to be picked up.
- Have you experienced rejection? Were you adopted or separated from a sibling? Were you wanted as a child or has someone let slip

that you were an 'accident'? Did your parents want a girl after three boys, or a boy after several girls?

- Have you ever experienced feeling unworthy when you were younger? Perhaps you were picked on for being too fat or too thin? Maybe you were bullied or teased? Perhaps you were always taking the blame for your sibling's mistakes?
- Have you ever experienced physical or mental abuse of any kind?

The Past Is Not the Present

The reason I mention all of this is so you can begin to make a distinction between the feelings you have right now and feelings from the past. It's tough enough going through your break-up in the present; it's even tougher if you are adding old hurts to the mix. Another question I want you to ask yourself every time you have an 'emotional hit' that raises your emotional temperature is: 'What does this feeling remind me of'?

You may have to think this question over for a while before the answer comes to you.

If it reminds you of the past, I want you to make a clear distinction for yourself: *This is not that, and then is not now.*

This is a vital distinction to make, because if your feelings are connected with the past, there may be some unresolved upsets that need addressing. Muddling the past and the present creates more chaos in your mind. What you need is clarity. Your relationship break-up gives you an opportunity to explore what's true for you right now. Through the fog of your feelings, the big question is 'What are the reasons for my relationship break-up?'

The answer may have more to do with specific expectations that you had in your present relationship that were not fulfilled, than past situations or circumstances that were out of your control when you were young.

When you are able to make the distinction between now and then, you may even experience a 'light bulb' moment when you realize that your old beliefs may have been playing themselves out in your current relationship when actually they had nothing to do with this person and your life with them. We will explore this in more detail later on.

One of the most frustrating things about the pain of ending your relationship is the associated feelings and emotions that seem to beset you in the middle of the night or the early hours of the morning. It's a bit like in *The Godfather* when the movie producer Jack Woltz (played by John Marley) wakes up in bed with the horse's head on the pillow next to him. Our own personal horse's head is fear, guilt, panic, loneliness and sadness. If it happened to me, I'm pretty sure it will happen to you at some stage – and when it does I want you to be ready for it.

So here's a strategy. I mentioned it earlier, but here are the specifics.

Your Divorce Diary

I want you to begin to keep a journal by the side of your bed. Your Divorce Diary. The process of writing your thoughts down, removing them from your head and onto the paper is a proven therapeutic technique. You are already awake so you may as well do something useful. This is how you can set out your journal so that it works at any time of the day or night.

Use your journal at any time to write down your thoughts and especially if you have an uncomfortable feeling. Start each sentence with '**I feel …**' and continue until all your feelings are

---

on paper. The point is to transfer the feelings and emotions you carry around in your head on to paper. It helps to empty out your brain of its intense emotions.

After you feel complete and have nothing more to say, try the following exercise. This exercise is also particularly helpful if you wake up suddenly during the night.

Free Writing

Write down your immediate feeling and its accompanying emotion. Ask yourself: 'What is this trying to tell me?' 'What's the message?' Next ask yourself 'What action can I take to change the situation right now?' And lastly, 'What action can I take to help me right now?' You may want to have a page set out like this for immediate use.

Feeling	Emotion	What is this trying to tell me? What's the message?	What action can I take to change the situation right now?	What action can I take to help me right now?
Panic	Fear	I need to find out where I stand financially	Nothing as I am in bed and it's 4 a.m.!	Write down my worries so that I can call my lawyer tomorrow and ask questions

Get used to transferring your feelings into your journal. Your journal will also allow you to see how far you've travelled on your journey to recovery. Even after just a few weeks, you'll be pleasantly surprised at the progress you have made.

After Pain Comes Change

The quality and the timing of the changes you make after divorce depend entirely on you. Nothing is ever the same after a major loss in life. Without grieving for these losses and saying goodbye to what no longer applies to your life, it's harder to say hello to reconstructing your life on your terms. You *are* sad, you *are* angry, you *are* frightened, there's no point denying it. What I want you to know is that experiencing the pain that accompanies this crazy time in your life is absolutely vital. This painful process is the precursor to some amazing possibilities that will open up to you if you are willing to let go of anger and stop fighting with reality.

A year after she'd disappeared, Wendy came home. One day she just knocked at the door and Roy nearly had a heart attack on the spot. Of course he asked her in, and over a cup of tea Wendy tried to explain what had happened. She had woken up on the morning of her departure and realized that she was living a lie. She didn't know who she was or what she was doing living this life, and she just decided she had to get away. She knew that she would be hurting Roy, and part of her had wanted to do exactly that. She went first to see her doctor because she realized she might be having a breakdown. He saw her after surgery hours and gave her antidepressants, and she left for Brighton. She spent the first few weeks in a hotel, barely leaving her room except when she remembered she had to eat. She told the girls where she was but told them not to tell Roy.

The year passed in a haze of seafront walks, moving into a rented apartment and waiting for the fog inside her mind to lift. She realized that she had been living her life on automatic pilot and gradually started to understand how deeply unfulfilled she was. She also knew that it was so ungrateful not to appreciate all that she had had, but she just couldn't help wanting to find that elusive something that was missing from her life. As time went by she realized how dishonest she had been to herself, denying her own needs for personal fulfilment, meaningful work and making her own mark by using her talents and creativity. She began to work, writing for some local therapists who needed to publicize their practice and sending out press releases for local restaurants and shops. She didn't charge very much, but for the first time since she had met Roy she felt her identity return to her.

She had come back home to explain. She did not expect him to forgive her and she did not even know if she wanted to return or if he would want her. She just knew that her life had to be different from here onwards.

Roy asked Wendy if she would work with me, which she did. After several sessions we had a joint meeting with Roy to plan the way forward. Wendy moved into her own place nearer to Roy and they both decided to rebuild their relationship in a new fresh and honest way. They continue to work on a new way of being together. It's not always easy. They have had to learn how to communicate without fear, how to let each other have their own space and friends. Wendy says she has finally grown up and Roy realizes how much he took Wendy for granted. The pain they both endured was a precursor to enormous change for them both.

From Pain to Understanding

I have found that until people have been able to face their pain, it is very hard to get on with the rest of the healing process. Roy and Wendy are rebuilding their relationship; this was not an option for me and may not be for you either. But now that you are learning more about getting your feelings out into the open, it's time to get fully conscious and find out how you got to this place in your relationship. You are now ready to discover what happened, why it happened and how it was inevitable that you would end up where you are right now.

Personal Prescription for Your Intensive Care: Directions for Use

You are in 'intensive care' and need to take very good care of yourself. Every time your emotional temperature rises and painful thoughts come to mind, do not resist them. Instead, take a deep breath in and out. Calm yourself and then, in a loving way, ask your pain what it is trying to tell you. Listen for the answer, and then follow the 'Dosage' instructions.

Dosage

Write your feelings down in your Divorce Diary.

Once a day check to see where you are on the snakes and ladders game (see page 28).

As many times as you need to each day, practise your Thought Stopping (see page 30).

Self-Affirmation Medicine

The following affirmations must be repeated at least three times each, three times per day, for five consecutive days. As before, decide what times of day work best for you.

- It is comforting to know that I have all the necessary muscles I need to cope with really difficult times.
- I am taking one step at a time. That's how I will get where I am going.
- Today I will face and feel my fears because they will empower me to move on.
- Right now I have the will, strength and desire to continue working on my recovery.

Chapter 3
Regaining Consciousness

Awareness	Of your role in your relationship
Attitude	Choosing how you will deal with your emotions
Action	The most effective actions for responding rather than reacting

'All happy families are alike; every unhappy family is unhappy in its own way.' - **Leo Tolstoy**

How Did this Happen to Me?

When people sit down and settle in to work with me, they inevitably ask this question. It's really the most obvious question to begin with, and believe me there is an answer. I promise this isn't some weird plot against you. Actually, understanding why this happened is the most important stage in your recovery. It's vital that you gain awareness and wake up to your own role in this drama called divorce if you are to become conscious about how you got yourself into this situation. Your future happiness depends on it.

Does it sound like I'm putting the responsibility on you? Well, I am. At least partly. So let me explain why.

The Marriage Myth

'When two people are under the influence of the most violent,

most insane, most delusive and most transient of passions,
they are required to swear that they will remain in that
excited, abnormal and exhausting condition continuously
until death do them part.' **- George Bernard Shaw**

Our culture has very unrealistic ideas about marriage. It seems we are all expected somehow to navigate our own route to a happy marriage. Yet no one teaches us how to 'do' marriage. Yes, there are varying theories passed down from those who have managed to stay married for years and years. They recommend a large dose of compromise, keeping a sense of humour and knowing when to keep quiet, but even so it's all very vague.

Every marriage is bound to be as different as the people in it. Mostly our expectations are that marriage will enhance our life by sharing it with our soulmate. We'll have someone to create a future with, a family with and someone we'll be compatible and happy with. That's the ideal, and some of the time it delivers. But only *some* of the time.

Many of us falsely assume that our partners, once joined to us in matrimony, will be totally devoted to us, and us to them, and that a good marriage should be pretty much plain sailing.

Unfortunately, though, no one gives us an instruction manual or a toolkit to keep under the stairs to help us repair our relationship when things go wrong. We often don't even *know* when things are going wrong because we don't know what to look for. We certainly don't know how to talk to our partner to change their feelings or behaviour. We don't see the signs because we haven't been taught where to look. So what do we do? We get confused and defensive; we adapt our behaviours to suit our situation for the sake of a peaceful life; we compromise ourselves; we blame each other for what's going wrong or we withdraw from each other.

Because we don't know how to handle each other during times of upset, it's no surprise that many of our unrealistic ideas of marriage can easily be shattered and our relationship can go into meltdown. I've found that the great majority of people who get divorced can and do live in this cycle for many years before something catalytic happens, or the pain of remaining finally feels worse than the thought of leaving.

Of course, if our partner were different none of this would have happened. If only they were more like, well, like me! You've hit the nail on the head. You would completely understand them if they were more like you, but the reality is that they are not. They are who they are, and when who they are is unacceptable to you over a period of time, divorce offers a sure way out.

The Symptoms Below the Surface

I believe the symptoms of divorce lie dormant even before we get married. I really believe that the symptoms of divorce are incubating just below the surface, and the two main reasons are:

1. Marriage does not come with an operating manual.
2. We, as individuals, do not come with an operating manual.

Here's how it works.

If you don't know how *you* 'operate' on *every* level – which means you don't fully understand your needs and your values – and you decide to join forces with someone else who is also muddling through, then trial and error and a good deal of luck will become the foundations upon which you build your lives together. This worked fairly well when men ploughed the fields and women baked the bread, but we live in different times. Our roles are no longer defined by our gender. There are no clear-cut tasks or activities that are automatically apportioned any more.

When you combine our often-limited knowledge about ourselves with undefined marital ground rules, it's no wonder that marriage can become a breeding ground for the symptoms of divorce.

Old Wiring

There's almost an inevitability about what happened in your relationship. Even though 'it takes two' and you are partly responsible, it's probably not *consciously* your fault – and here's the reason why. Both your reactions and your interactions in your relationship are based on how you have been wired since birth. Everything you have ever seen, heard and absorbed, every day of your life, good and bad, is entered into your personal databank. As a result, you are who you are today.

Have you ever heard the expression 'Life isn't the way it is; it's the way we see it'? Well, that's exactly true. What happens out there in the world, every situation and every circumstance we find ourselves in, is viewed through our own personal lens. Our minds are always trying to find data that ties in with a previous experience, in order for us to make sense of what's happening now. Unless you are one of the few people who are fully conscious in the choices you make about everything you say or do, you are generally working from old data that you have built up over the years.

Your brain is like a personal computer that stores and files your 'what happened' data and never lets you forget it – at least subconsciously. You experience your life through your own personal reality of the world; for each of us, this becomes the truth about the way things are. Once it becomes your truth, you *behave* in alignment with your truth.

For example, if you have experienced life as being hard while you were growing up, and as an adult life is still pretty challenging, it would be fair to say that you will have entrenched the belief 'Life is hard.' One fine day you meet Sam. Sam has had a charmed childhood and continues to live a pretty charmed life. For him 'Life is a ball.' Who is telling the truth? Neither is right or wrong. It's the same country, the same year, the same day. But each sees 'life' through his or her own lens, and lives it accordingly.

Lucy and David's Story

Lucy, a 36-year-old stay-at-home mum with four children under seven, doesn't understand why her toy-laden house and finger-marked walls drive David so mad. She never ceases to be amazed when he shouts at her about discipline and nags the children to tidy up. She certainly does not take his admonishments seriously. She loves nothing more than paint pots and plasticine all around as the children play happily and noisily in almost every room in the house. She doesn't mind food on the sofa or crumbs on the carpet. Why on earth doesn't David understand that it's not possible to keep the home as perfect as it was before the kids came along? Why would you even want to?

Lucy grew up with an alcoholic mother. As the oldest girl with two brothers she was playing the role of mum by eight years old, because more often than not her mother would be drunk by the time Lucy got home from school. Dad worked longer and longer hours as Lucy grew up. She knew he didn't really need to, he just didn't want to come home, but she was grateful that at least he didn't abandon them all completely.

Lucy longed for a normal family like her best friend Jess had. Jess's mum baked cakes, played Scrabble and was always available for a hug. Their house was what you would call 'lived in'. No one worried too much about clearing up, but boy, did they have fun. Lucy made a promise to herself that one day she would have a family just like Jess's.

David, on the other hand, comes from a family of nine children. Their small house meant that David shared his bedroom with three brothers and space was extremely limited. In their town, where many people were out of work for years on end, it was a real struggle to feed and clothe everyone and there certainly wasn't much 'quality' time with Mum. However, she always managed to keep their less-than-lovely home pristine. Everyone helped each other and respected how hard Mum and Dad worked. It would not have occurred to David to make life even more difficult than it already was by making a mess.

Now David and Lucy argue constantly. Both of them come from their own perspectives and neither can understand the other. David feels thoroughly disrespected by Lucy and upset that the older children don't take him seriously either. He cannot understand how Lucy can allow such wayward behaviour in their beautiful home that he personally built himself. Lucy simply wants their children to have a real home and is thoroughly bored with David's constant nagging, which, by the way, has now progressed to include mostly everything she does and mostly everything she says to him. Their marriage is currently at stalemate. Lucy says she doesn't even recognize David any more.

Do I Know You?

If you get nothing else out of this book but this one golden nugget, it is that the reason most people divorce is that *they have never really met each other.* They are not in relationship with each other, they are in relationship with their past conditioning – and the decisions and choices they made were based on what they have experienced. Lucy and David have been hard-wired by their conditioning. Here's Lucy determined to provide her children with the kind of home that she didn't have so that she can heal her past. There's David determined to keep a home that's pristine to prove that his parents did their best and nothing was missing for him.

This is not Lucy and David in relationship. This is both their old wirings in relationship.

Now stay with me on this one, because understanding how the old wiring shows up in daily life means first understanding the *specific* old wirings that Lucy and David have held on to from their past.

Lucy's Old Wiring

Lucy never felt really loved by her mum (from the age of about six onwards) because her mum was inebriated most of the time. She had to look after her brothers and sisters and never really had a childhood of her own. She longed for a home life like her friend's. Lucy's old wiring is called *'I'm not loved enough.'*

David, on the other hand, realized (from about the age of seven) that you work hard for what you have and then you take great care of it. He had to be responsible for everything he had and everything he did. Plus he realized that everyone needed to be pulling together to have the best life possible. David's old wiring is called *'I have to be responsible.'*

Lucy has gone through her life doing whatever she can to be loved. This means she has turned a blind eye to hurts and personal upsets so that she can avoid any conflict that would detract from her being loved. She remains cheerful at all times and smiles a lot. She just wants David to love her.

David has gone through life believing that it's important to take responsibility for who you are and what you do. His success in life comes from taking responsibility and being acknowledged for his achievements. His parents are so proud of him. He wants Lucy to respect and acknowledge him for what he does.

When Lucy met David she was easy-going and playful. She paid a great deal of attention to David and he loved her free spirit and laughter. It allowed him to relax in a way that had not been possible before.

In turn, Lucy loved David's personal strength, his sense of responsibility and his desire to build a wonderful home for their family. This was something she had longed for. Perfect! Except something went wrong.

When they argue about the state of the house, David feels disrespected by Lucy's reaction to his requests. He quite forgets that the very qualities that made him fall in love with Lucy in the first place are now the ones he most dislikes. In turn, when David criticizes and nags, Lucy feels unloved. It skips her mind that she fell in love with his sense of responsibility and strength. What she didn't understand was that his version of a wonderful home for the family would look very different to hers.

David and Lucy are in turmoil, yet surprisingly they both get something out of holding on to their old wiring. The whole structure of their individual worlds would change if they were to let go of the old wiring. To let go would mean that they would have to do something else instead, something different, and what would that be? Scary stuff, but on the other hand how much does it cost them to maintain their old wiring?

Taking 100 per cent responsibility for your old wiring is huge. It means you have to admit that by operating in alignment with it you have played a role in the demise of your relationship. As I said earlier, most people are quite unconscious of their old wiring; that's why so many relationships are cast to the winds without one or the other really understanding why. Couples who are able to have a 'happy' divorce (a divorce without drama) are those who piece together the puzzle and realize that, given how they both operated in the relationship, it could not have turned out any other way. At this point it's clear that blaming each other is pointless and totally futile.

Old Wiring in a Relationship

Lucy's Stuck Record *'I'm not loved enough'*	David's Stuck Record *'I have to be responsible'*
Benefit I get to be right and I can give you examples, such as if David really loved me he would understand how important it is to me to have a happy, easy-going home for the kids. I get to avoid having to say 'no' to the children and setting boundaries because, if I did, they might not love me. I get to avoid taking 100 per cent responsibility for my own life, because, if I did, I might have to risk not being loved, which is unthinkable.	**Benefit** I get to be right and I can give you examples, such as if Lucy really respected me she would understand how important it is to me to have a tidy home. I get to avoid letting go of control because, if I did, things might fall apart and I would not be being responsible. I get to avoid taking 100 per cent responsibility for my own life, because, if I did, I might have to risk being irresponsible, and that would be unthinkable.
Cost Holding on to my stuck record costs me: my relationship with David, being true to myself and having personal boundaries in place without worrying that I will not be loved.	**Cost** Holding on to my stuck record costs me: my relationship with Lucy, being free and relaxed and having fun without having to take responsibility for everything.

How Old Are You Really?

It's important to reiterate that your old wiring and its accompanying behaviours were anchored at an early age, generally between 5 and 15. This was the time when you constructed your own personal reality based on what you observed around you and how you could best fit in to your surroundings. If it's important to 'be responsible', you construct behaviours that support that. If it's important to 'be loved', you most certainly find the ways and means of getting that need met. However, the behaviours you constructed at an early age are simply not appropriate for use as fully grown adults. When you were a child these behaviours served you well. First you got a great pay-off for behaving 'that' way. Secondly, because you were in survival mode, you made decisions based on the mental resources you had available at the time and behaved in a way that you felt served you best.

However, for Lucy and David to behave like seven-year-olds when they are both well into their 30s doesn't work. They may have grown into adults but their emotional ages stayed rooted in childhood. This means that every time they feel an 'emotional hit' and each of their emotional temperatures rises, they react like seven-year-olds. They revert to their old wiring and they argue from an emotional age of seven.

By the way, there are of course many more costs for you when you hang on to your old wiring. This way of operating doesn't just play itself out in your personal relationships; it may also have implications in other areas of your life, for example in your work and with your friends. You may come to realize that when you react emotionally outside your relationship it's still the small child inside you trying to justify or defend its position. Growing older does not always bring emotional maturity, either. I know people of 80 who are still reacting like 12-year-olds.

Fusing the System

In order to understand why many marriages fail, it's clear that a good place to start is by looking below the surface to see how people are wired up.

Whatever has led you to this place, whether you are choosing to leave the relationship or you have been left, it has happened as a result of who you have been up to this point in your life. Because you've continued to operate with old wiring, your whole system has fused. The opportunity for you now is to get super-conscious about how you've operated in the past so that you can choose a different route for your future.

Self-examination

I'd like you to complete the following exercise. By examining yourself in this way you will discover your own personal old wiring. This will give you a heightened awareness of how you operate in a relationship.

Regaining full consciousness is about waking up to yourself and learning how your role in your relationship contributed to its demise. While this may be a difficult and confrontational exercise, I suggest you find yourself a quiet place to sit down, take a deep breath and work through it. It may well be the most important piece of soul-searching you have ever undertaken, and one that will create lasting clarity regarding your relationship.

I believe that unless you understand how your old wiring impacts on how you behave in relationship, you will continue to react to people, situations and circumstances as you have always done. In the future your new-found awareness will give you back the power of choice so that you have the opportunity to *choose* how you want to behave instead of reacting on automatic pilot.

The Stuck Record

Think back to a time in the past when you first had thoughts that began with any of the statements listed below. There may be a few that apply to you because none of us has just one 'stuck record'. Many of us have quite a few. Choose the one that's most prevalent, the one that pops into your mind most regularly.

- I should (I should be thinner/I should be quieter)
- I mustn't be (I mustn't be so loud/I mustn't be so enthusiastic/I mustn't be selfish)
- I must (I must be a good boy/I must be reliable/I must be there when needed/I must be looked after/I must be responsible)
- I have to (I have to keep quiet/I have to be the joker/I have to take care of them/I have to look after myself/I have to do everything)
- I can't (I can't be true to myself/I can't do what others do/I can't do it on my own/I can't find love)
- I don't (I don't fit in/I don't look right/I don't get what I want)
- I'll never (I'll never have what I want/I'll never fit in)
- I'm not (I'm not clever enough/I'm not brave enough/I'm not sure/I'm not good enough)

The Benefit

There is always a benefit to staying in the groove of your 'stuck record'. If there were no benefits, you'd have changed the record long ago. However ironic these appear to be, believe me, these benefits keep the needle in the groove and stop you from moving forward.

The formula always begins with: *'I get to be right and I can give you examples.'*

You might say, 'I'm right that I am not good enough. After all, I didn't pass my driving test first time, I wasn't ever picked for the team, I don't earn enough money.'

Give some examples to justify your own stuck record.

'I am right that I ... and I can give you examples like the time when ...'

Then there's the added bonus of **'what I get to avoid by holding on to this thought and making it into a belief.'**

For example, if you believe you're not good enough, you get to avoid:

- trying anything out of my comfort zone in case I fail
- putting myself in a position where I may experience the pain of rejection in a relationship, at work and in following my dreams

Write down, 'I get to avoid ...' and fill in your blanks.

Now complete the formula with this statement: *'I get to avoid taking 100 per cent responsibility for my own life because ...'*

When we take 100 per cent responsibility for our lives in our relationships, we say and do things very differently. Think of your own situation: Where have you held back? When have you taken your foot off the gas? How have you behaved that allowed your ex-partner to behave in the way they did?

Do some soul-searching and ask yourself where you have avoided taking 100 per cent responsibility. Is it possible you are still doing it now? (If not in your relationship, in another area of your life?)

This is a powerful self-examination exercise and you will need some time to reflect on what you have learned. When I do this work with individuals and couples, the realization that their past has had such an impact on their present evokes a variety of emotions. Not only that, but when they realize that they were *married to someone else's past*, it takes a little time to digest the impact this has had on their relationship.

So be kind to yourself. Back there, then, you did the very best you could with the resources you had available to you. Your stuck record was able to protect you and keep you safe when you needed it. As a result of what you decided about yourself and your life, you were able to create behaviours that were vital to your survival and growth. There may be some behaviours that you still want to retain, like being responsible, being generous or being funny. Please do so. Just make sure it's on your terms and not because you believe it's expected of you.

Before you make any decisions, though, let's take a closer look at your behaviour in relationship.

Our Individual Learned Behaviours

As a result of our old wiring, there are some learned behaviours that we all bring to marriage and long-term relationships. These behaviours have the power to dictate whether a relationship will work from the outset.

That's quite a statement to make. You may find it hard to believe, so let me say it another way. We have all learned how to behave in order to get our needs met. We bring these learned behaviours with us when we go into relationship. Some people have quite fixed behaviours and are determined to hold on to them. This means that these people will display behaviours that may have served them well when they were younger and single, but will be challenging to their partner in relationship. These people often manage to find partners who are adaptable enough to let them get their own way most, if not all, of the time.

Some people can adapt their behaviours more easily than others. They are more flexible and are good at compromise. Some people have realized at some point in their lives that being able to adapt serves them pretty well in getting their needs met. They've learned how to get the best for themselves by co-operating with others.

Some other people have learned to be very malleable indeed. These are generally the 'people-pleasers'. They will mould their behaviour to suit every situation. They appear to be pushovers. The truth is that this is just another learned behaviour which they have found effective in getting their need to be loved met.

The reality is that we all have the ability to manifest all these types of behaviour, but we have decided, through circumstance, situation and culture, to exhibit more of one and less of another most of the time. It's no coincidence, though, that our behaviour patterns attract us to people who will *allow* us to continue to behave in our own way.

Choosing Our 'Perfect Partner'

For the most part, we unconsciously choose partners who will accommodate and complement our most obvious behaviours. In Transactional Analysis, a therapy created by Eric Berne, he cites that our most obvious behaviours fall into three 'ego states': Parent, Adult and Child. Berne felt that we relate to each other and communicate with each other from these three positions. Here's how it works:

1. Parent Behaviours

- Over-responsible
- Critical/judgemental
- Caring
- Controlling

2. Adult Behaviours

- Independent/self-reliant
- Create win-win situations
- Fully self-expressed
- Respected and respectful

3. Child Behaviours

- Need validation
- Under-responsible
- Not self-reliant
- Defensive

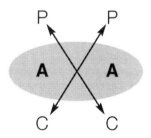

Parent/Adult/Child interaction: You don't want you and your ex to relate as Parent–Child or Child–Parent. Adult to Adult is the level of communication to strive for.

Take a good look at the behaviours in each position. This is not a comprehensive list, just the most common behaviours manifested in each position. Do you recognize any of them? How do you react if your partner speaks to you when he or she is in the Parent position? Perhaps you answer back like a defensive Child? Perhaps you counter-respond as your partner's Parent? The question is, how often do you, or did you, respond as an Adult?

Most of the time when we are in relationship meltdown, we are relating to each other as Parent to Child, Child to Parent, Child to Child or Parent to Parent. In relationship meltdown, even if we attempt to relate to our partner from our Adult, the response we receive in return will probably not come from our partner's Adult position. When you combine your years of internal wiring with the behaviours they produce, and on top of all that relate to your partner as a Parent or a Child, the results are disastrous.

One night several months after my own divorce I was struck by this phenomenon even though I didn't know there was a proven formula for it. I had just completed the second day of a three-day personal development course and it suddenly occurred to me what my role might have been in my own marriage. I called my ex-husband at 1 a.m. and asked him if he would come over as I had something I wanted to say to him. Strangely he said he would.

When he arrived I kept him on the doorstep and said to him, 'Do you think it's possible that all through our marriage you related to me as your mother and I related to you as my father?' While he was not into any personal growth work himself, he immediately understood what I was saying, and agreed. As the full realization of my words hit me, I then carried on, 'So it's possible that we were never Mark and Francine at all. We were just playing these unconscious roles as each other's parents.' He agreed and we just stood looking at each other while we let this sink in, and then he went home.

It was a bizarre yet catalytic conversation. Although this had not been the only reason for our relationship meltdown, I could see immediately how it had been an underlying symptom from the very beginning. When I looked back to our courtship, he had been the 'parent' and I had started our relationship as the 'needy child'. It was not until we'd got married that I changed roles and often played parent instead.

So what about your role and behaviours? Just for a moment, take a look at your own relationship and ask yourself honestly …

- Which role did I play or do I still play in my relationship?
- What specific behaviours do I adopt that I feel help me to survive?
- What behaviours have I learned that I would rather 'unlearn'?
- How has my behaviour affected my relationship?
- Do I know why I behave the way I do?
- How did my ex-partner behave? How does he/she behave now?

You are probably beginning to see that the symptoms of relationship breakdown run deep. As you read this I'm aware that you may still be hurting. We still have a way to go before you achieve your happy divorce. However, I hope that understanding a bit more about the underlying symptoms that have led you to this place in your life has created a greater awareness of how it all happened. They say knowledge is power if you know how to use it, and the more powerful you feel during the weeks to come, the more strength you will have to cope with what lies ahead.

What *Does* Lie Ahead?

One of the things that certainly lies ahead is coping with your ex-partner. In order for you to heal your heart and move forward with your life, you will need to be able to handle your ex and the ways she or he may affect you in the weeks and months to come. Now that you understand your feelings and some of the reasons why your break-up was inevitable, you have a good foundation as you approach the Ex Files. But before you do, please first take your Regaining Consciousness prescription.

Personal Prescription for the Symptoms of Divorce: Directions for Use

You are required to put yourself under observation. Your prescription is an opportunity for you to choose how to 'be'. This is about choosing your attitude. At this stage of your treatment, I want to raise your awareness and help you become fully conscious of your situation. I want you to begin to discover for yourself what might stand in the way of your healing, and begin to understand the behaviours that will best serve you as you start the road to recovery.

Dosage

When you have answered the questions below, I'd like you to refer back to them twice a day for the next five days. Feel free to make any changes to your answers on a daily basis. Keep a note of your emotions in your Divorce Diary each time you read through the questions.

- Taking away all blame, what's the reality of my personal situation right now?
- Taking away all blame or guilt, what am I resisting?
- How do I feel when I resist?
- How do I behave as a result?
- How would I prefer to behave?
- How would I benefit from behaving that way?

Self-Affirmation Medicine

The following affirmations must be repeated at least 10 times each, three times per day, for five consecutive days.

- I will face my fears courageously today.
- Today, I am responsible for my reactions and behaviours.
- I am gaining emotional strength every day.

Part Two
Recuperation

Chapter 4
The Ex Files

In this chapter we'll look at the following:

Awareness	Of what it means to emotionally divorce
Attitude	Choosing the language and behaviours that serve your emotional divorce
Action	Taking the actions that allow you to emotionally separate

Filing Away Your Ex

During my own divorce I had a specific file for all my husband's correspondence. I called it, naturally enough, 'The Ex Files'. Every time I allocated a piece of necessary documentation or unnecessary nonsense that passed between us to the Ex Files, it felt like I was able to put my feelings outside myself into a manila folder which I kept in the garage. I thought if I distanced myself from the offending emails, letters and notes that I would feel better and heal faster. This physical act of detachment was supposed to create emotional detachment.

If only it was that easy!

If only we could just file away all our feelings and emotions connected to our ex-partners without them finding their way out of a locked outhouse and back into our breaking hearts.

Obviously, taking down the photos of the two of you together and hiding your wedding album helps, but the pictures and old movies we run in our heads are much harder to hide away. At some point or another, we have to come to terms with emotionally divorcing ourselves from our partners.

Your emotional divorce simply doesn't happen overnight. Even if you are feeling the liberation that leaving a partner who has caused you pain and hurt brings, it's unlikely that you have done all the work needed to divorce *emotionally*. It's only when you can run those old movies in your head without feeling bitterness and anger that you are really on the way to finalizing your emotional separation.

The Emotional Divorce

It's rare for me to work with couples who have come to the decision *together* to divorce. Often, one partner had already made the decision to leave and had probably left 'emotionally' months or even years prior to their actual announcement. This means the other partner has quite a bit of work to do to catch up and begin their own process of Emotionally Divorcing.

You'll be able to identify an ex who has already 'left the building' by the following characteristics:

- They are uncommunicative.
- They are distant and cold.
- They find reasons to spend less time at home.
- They are impatient and often irritable.
- When they ask for a divorce they want it to happen as quickly as possible.

Conversely, the person being left often exhibits some of these characteristics:

- Shock and denial. He or she hadn't realized that there were problems in the marriage.
- Looking for ways to save the marriage by asking questions like 'Tell me what didn't I do?' or 'What else could I have done?'
- Can humiliate themselves by begging for another chance.
- May exhibit strange behaviours such as playing detective and following their spouse in their car, gathering evidence of affairs or generally just haranguing them on a daily basis.
- Expresses feelings of deep anxiety and fear about the future.
- May try to do anything they can to delay the divorce process.

From these lists it would be easy to conclude that it's the person who has been left who causes most of the emotional conflict and punishing behaviours, but oftentimes the leaver has been so frustrated for such a long time that their behaviour, which can include verbal accusations or abuse or volatile outbursts, is just as unacceptable as their partner's.

For most people, this stage is the hardest part of divorce. You are confronted with the reality of your situation, and for many people their ex-spouse now becomes the enemy. Swords are drawn and battle begins. All the feelings we looked at in Chapter 2 are exposed like open wounds, and any and all behaviours and communications can be easily misconstrued.

The one who has been left will try to control the leaver by means of manipulation and guilt-inducing behaviours as they try to come to terms with their perceived betrayal and deception. They will try to pull their partner back from the brink because the fear and emotional pain they are feeling are too much to bear.

The leaver will resist and continue to be frustrated by the punishing behaviour of their ex, and the more this provoking behaviour continues, the more they have good reason to want out of the relationship.

Try telling either party that these self-defeating behaviours are unnecessary and all you will hear is one story after another of justification and blame.

It's Not about You!

In order to exert some control over your emotions, it's important to understand a simple – but perhaps hard to swallow – fact: the person you are divorcing (or who is divorcing you) is *not* an evil person, however unacceptable their actual behaviours may be. There are very few truly evil souls. We know that most people are a product of their conditioning, give or take a few rogue genes. So it's unlikely that your ex woke up one morning and said to themselves something like, 'How can I best hurt Lucy today? Oh, I know, I'll spend all our money on my addiction or make some really bad business decisions or I'll sleep with another woman.' When they were spending the money or sleeping with someone else, or whatever behaviour they were manifesting, you can be sure they were thinking *purely about themselves*. You didn't even figure in their thoughts. They were not wondering or caring about the impact their behaviour would have on you. Nor were they doing what they were doing to get back at you in some way. They were simply attending to their own wants and needs.

Imagining that this person set out specifically to hurt you is completely missing the point, and it's exactly this way of thinking that makes the situation much more painful than it already is. **It's not about you!** As I have said, previously, yes, it's true that you are affected, deeply, by their behaviour, but the moment you go into your head and into your ego and make up that they did whatever they did to hurt *you*, you are on a one-way street to nowhere.

Long before the actual event or series of events that amounted to the 'last straw' happened, there would have been subtle cues and clues that indicated that being in the relationship was not working for them any more. Unable to express their dissatisfaction for whatever reason – perhaps because they believed you would not understand them or even care, or they were afraid of the consequences, or the guilt they already felt (the list is endless) – they simply were not able to articulate their concerns. Now they are looking for a way to distance themselves from all the hurt and pain. (Conversely, if you are the one instigating the break-up, you will know how this applies to you.)

Behaving with Dignity

There are ways of handling yourself in this situation that work, and ways that just give you more pain and frustration. If you think you can control your ex with irrational and unacceptable behaviour you will certainly be banging your head against the proverbial brick wall. The wisest thing you can do is realize that *you only have control over yourself and your own emotions*. Only by focusing on controlling your *own* emotions will you be able to move effectively through the process of your emotional divorce and emerge with your dignity and identity intact, as well as making it easier for you to parent effectively and navigate your way through the legal and practical process of divorce.

> *When you are able to view yourself as a separate individual and no longer your ex's partner, the process of emotionally divorcing will finally be complete.*

So how can this be achieved?

Separating Mentally and Physically – The Real Drama of Divorce

In the words of the song, 'Breaking up is hard to do.' When a long-term relationship ends, most people will agree that separating mentally as well as physically from your ex can be a very challenging process. Very many people experience the one-foot-in-and-one-foot-out stage of oscillating back and forth as they try to extricate themselves from all the tentacles that bind them to their partner. And believe me, there are *many* tentacles. Some couples can spend anything from several months to several years trying to liberate themselves from the hold their partners seemingly have over them, or from the drama of entanglements and complications that keep them from escaping from a comfortless and joyless marriage.

Emily and Tom's Story

Married for five years, both had a child from a previous marriage: Casey, age seven, was Emily's daughter; George, nine, was Tom's son. Both children live with them. Sadly, Tom's former wife had been killed while riding her bicycle. It hadn't been anyone's fault – she had caught her trouser leg in a pedal, swerved to release it and fallen off her bicycle in front of a car. Tom was devastated and never imagined he would ever love again. But one year later, Tom met Emily in the local doctor's surgery. They began chatting, and developed a friendship. Emily was kind and understanding, and became a lifesaver for Tom and George. In turn, Emily admired Tom for being such a great father to George and doing so much for him. How very different to Emily's ex-husband, who had participated very little in the childcare.

After a short courtship, Emily agreed to marry Tom. Because she had learned a great deal about what she wanted in relationship from her previous marriage, she was able to discuss the ground rules with Tom about how they would run their home and family. One small problem: Tom didn't keep to the rules. Shortly after they were married he began to complain how tired he was and how work was so stressful. He participated less and less, and Emily realized that she was experiencing the same patterns that had ended her former relationship. She was taking care of everyone, doing everything and getting little back in return from Tom. She tackled Tom about it, but he always had a reason for not contributing to the household chores and for not making more time for Emily and the family.

Eventually Tom agreed to go to counselling with Emily, but Emily never really felt they were given the right tools to deal with their conflicts. The rift between them expanded. Unable to live with the situation, Emily left with her daughter Casey, who was three at the time, but came back after a few days because Casey missed George and George missed Emily. Emily realized that she was emotionally tied to Tom through his son. Her compassion for George having lost his mother meant that she could not possibly allow him to lose yet another mum. She loved George very much, but her love for Tom was waning.

This pattern continued for several years. When Emily became overwhelmed and drained by the situation at home, she would leave for a week or so, but would always come back. Tom would be helpful and considerate for a short while and then he would revert back to form and the relationship would start to wind down again.

When Emily came to see me she had come to the end of the road. She wanted to divorce Tom, but there was a further major problem. Emily had been stunned by Tom's recent revelation that he had MS. He had been diagnosed before they'd married, but had never told Emily. He had only experienced mild symptoms during the course of their marriage and had kept it well hidden, hiding behind excuses of tiredness and stress at work. Three months previously he had woken up one morning and not been able to walk very well, and things had gone from bad to worse. He'd had to tell Emily his secret.

She was furious. How could he have kept this from her? What kind of a man was he? She was frightened and angry and trapped. Tom had been too scared to tell her. He knew how selfish he had been but he truly did love her and always had. However, he thought that if he had revealed his condition, she might have had second thoughts about marrying him. His MS was the reason why he had been unable to help her more and why he had been too tired to participate with the family and be there for her.

For Emily this was too much too late. Now Tom was getting to the stage where walking was becoming difficult and his body was just not co-operating with his mind. He would soon need a wheelchair permanently. He could no longer work and was on sickness benefits, and although Emily had a very well-paying job, she was now working twice as hard to keep her job and take care of the family and Tom. How could she leave him when he was in this situation? She was incredibly angry that he had never let her know, frustrated that she hadn't left earlier and had ended up living with a man she didn't love who needed her more than ever.

It was so hard for Emily to decide to let go and not sacrifice her life for Tom. It took many months of agonizing soul-searching for her to come to her decision. She worked with me, her local minister, Tom's doctor and finally she admitted she could no longer stay married to Tom. It had nothing to do with his illness; she had fallen out of love with him years previously but her to-ing and fro-ing and indecision had meant that by the time she was ready to leave, circumstances beyond her control had simply taken over. After many painful conversations, it was agreed that Emily would leave and that George would live with her and Casey.

Emily and I began to put the mental and physical boundaries in place that Emily would need for her own survival in order to emotionally divorce Tom.

Working with Emily, we used various strategies that I'll discuss later in this chapter. First, we need to look at a game that Emily and Tom – and so many couples – play, called 'collusion'.

The Game of Collusion

In cases where the person you are leaving has an addiction or is suffering from any kind of illness, or even if they are experiencing career or business problems, it's normal to have some feelings of responsibility and guilt about ending the relationship. You may believe that leaving them is like kicking a person when they are down. How could you be that selfish? And if you are that person yourself, it's so hard not to feel abandoned, rejected, judged and scared.

> Staying with someone because you believe they are powerless to cope without you is unfair to them and to you.

You may ask how this is unfair to the person you are leaving. Good question. The reason is that by experiencing them as powerless you send them the message that they cannot cope without you. You are judging that, without you, their world will fall apart and they'll end up in a heap on the pavement. If that's what you believe and you stay for that reason, then they will *never* have a chance to do what needs to be done to take care of themselves. ***You collude with them to take away their personal responsibility for their own growth and the opportunity for them to find creative resources inside themselves that will allow their own personal development.***

The reason that your partner behaves the way they do, and has behaved this way in your relationship, is because they can. The more you turn yourself inside out trying to be or do what you think they need you to be or do, the more their behaviour will persist.

There are no winners in the collusion game. Both of you lose and neither of you grows. The co-dependency that you create, which you dress up as 'unselfishness' or 'guilt', only keeps you both from becoming so much more than you are. This is a dangerous game.

I often ask my clients, 'Why do you think some men and women beat up their spouses?' People have all kinds of different answers. They say it's about power, control or ignorance. Actually, there is only one reason: People who beat their partners do so simply *because they can.*

Let me explain. If you were to beat me up every night, and one night you came home from work and I was no longer there, could you beat me up? Of course not, because I would not be around to be your punchbag. If I stay, I am virtually giving you permission to beat me. Having worked with women whose partners abused them, I know that it's exceptionally difficult to have the courage to leave. When you have someone telling you in actions and words that this is what you deserve, you can come to believe it. When there is nowhere else to go and children and finances get in the way, it seems like you are trapped and cannot get out. There are some desperately sad situations that I know of, and all of us have read horrific stories of mental and physical abuse in the press. But, in the end, everyone in this situation has to leave and take refuge elsewhere to save their own lives.

Hopefully you will never experience anything as terrible as this, but *colluding with any behaviour* that your partner manifests that is impacting and affecting your own life just means the behaviour will continue. Eventually you must make a stand and say enough is enough.

Your Situation

Your own situation may have certain similarities to Emily and Tom's. You may be connected in ways that make it very difficult to remove yourself from your relationship even though you know it's not serving you any more. It may be that you both work in the family business which relies upon both your talents to keep an income flowing. Maybe you are still so physically attracted to your partner that this has allowed you to overlook their obvious shortcomings for so long. Perhaps your partner is a depressive and has been for years. Maybe you have tried to find ways to help them but nothing has worked. Perhaps you are connected by children from previous relationships and have become a step-parent, or it may be that you are just plain scared to let go. But there comes a time when you have to say enough is enough. You simply have to let go.

The Ego Mind

If I were to tell you that there is only one thing that stops you from letting go of your partner, whether you are the leaver or the leavee, you may find it quite challenging to take on board. But here goes.

> *What stops you from separating mentally and physically from your partner are your **thoughts** about who you are, can be, do or have **without** your partner.*

And, every single one of those individual thoughts is held in a vice-like grip by the CEO of your mind, your ego.

Please be clear that I don't mean ego in the 'big headed' sense. I mean it in the mind sense. Your ego is the *conscious identity* that you have created for yourself.

Let me explain. Your ego has nothing to do with who you really are, or who any of us really is in essence. It's the identity that you created for yourself, probably around the age of five, when you started to make sense of the world around you and gave yourself a structure around which to live your life. Being ego-driven means that you are driven by the thoughts and beliefs you have about the way 'it'/'life' is for you, based on data that you have collected over the years.

Because your ego is so greedy for validation of its existence, and feels safer and more righteous if other people agree with your beliefs about the way life should look and be, you project your rules for life onto someone else. If your partner does not honour your rules, it feels like they have invalidated you as a person. It's as if they have invalidated your identity. It's your ego mind that tells you how right you are and how obviously wrong they are for not being able to do and be what you want them to be.

We all do this. If we knew how to do it differently, we would. But not many of us have an alternative. We are literally controlled by our ego minds.

The ego mind is not a bad thing if you understand it. It's just that, sometimes, if it gets overworked and overwhelmed, it has the ability to take us down the route of paranoia or depression. That's why it's so important to be aware of it and not believe everything it tells you.

The Gremlin's Voice – Sabotage and Alert

The ego mind is like having a gremlin on your shoulder that doesn't shut up even at night. It keeps you awake but it tires you out, and rarely gives you a moment's peace to think clearly.

The ego mind doesn't mean to be nasty – in fact, one of its main purposes is to keep you safe and maintain the status quo. It hates change. So every time you think about leaving your unhappy relationship or being left by your partner, or even taking a huge leap of faith into the unknown, your ego mind will gather as many of its gremlin friends together as it can find and have an outrageous rave in your head.

To combat this, you have to begin to make some very astute distinctions. Is your ego mind trying to alert you to something you *should* know about? Is there something you have missed that may negatively affect you? Or is it plainly sabotaging you with thoughts that don't serve you in any way except to upset you even more?

It's exceptionally difficult to put the ego mind on hold for long. The great sages and seekers, the yoga gurus, the Zen masters and probably the Dalai Lama have perhaps cracked it, but my belief is that living in a material world, where 99.9 per cent of us are mind-driven and our 'spirits' dwell in human overcoats, it's not possible for even the most enlightened of us to put our ego minds on hold all of the time.

We can, however, all become masters of our ego minds and thoughts for brief periods of time. When you understand how to do this, and with daily practice during this difficult time, you'll make a huge difference to the way you react to and feel about your ex, in a way that is hard to imagine right now.

Your ego mind plays two prominent roles inside your head: the Saboteur and the Alerter.

Take a look at this strategy. It's one I have been working with for many years which addresses these two roles and which gives great results.

The Saboteur Strategy

The Saboteur way of thinking is self-defeating and says things like 'I'll never be loved again.' You cannot absolutely, beyond a shadow of doubt, know that this is true. But when you hold on to this kind of thought, how do you react? What do you experience inside your body and how do you ultimately feel as a result of this kind of thought? If the answer is pretty lousy, then the Saboteur is at work.

It's true that you may never be loved again by your ex, but as long as you are here on this earth there is the possibility that out of all the billions of people on the planet someone might find it in their heart to love you. Of course you won't be able to stay inside your home for the rest of your life and hide, but when you are ready to let someone else into your life, it's more than likely that after kissing several frogs or frogesses, you'll find someone else to share your life with. To think otherwise is pure sabotage that keeps you small and scared.

The Alert Strategy

The Alert Strategy is like an alarm bell that goes off in your head. It's a warning that needs attention; ignore it at your peril. Your ex says 'I'm going to take the kids and live in Australia.' This could be a threat in order to negotiate some favourable deal, or it could be their true intention. Whatever the truth for your ex, this is no time to wallow in emotional thoughts about what this means to you as a parent. Recognize the alert and immediately seek out the people who can advise you of your rights. Once you have the information and you have discovered that your ex cannot move abroad without your permission, the alert will turn off. You will have done your homework and the gremlins can go bother another troubled soul.

Confusing the Two Strategies

OK, so you know your rights regarding your children and you've had a flirty chat with someone at work. You are therefore both fanciable and still in a position to parent your kids – problems over. However, the gremlins are still delivering 'What if?' thoughts like 'What if I go out with X and my ex wants me back?' Or 'What if my kids want to live with my ex?' We're back with the Saboteur. Because once you have addressed the true 'alert' thoughts and they are taken care of, any remaining fleeting thoughts are just sabotaging you from moving on with your life.

The bad news is that you'll probably be having these conversations in your head for the rest of your life, but the good news is that when you practise making a distinction between sabotage and alert you'll notice how differently you respond to your thoughts. Understanding the difference gives you choice. When you have a choice, you feel much more in control of your own mind and, when you get really good at it, you'll experience a sense of freedom and liberation as you wave the gremlins goodbye and step out into the world and grow.

Change Your Thoughts

How else can you control those sabotaging thoughts so that you can change the whole way you react emotionally to your ex? A strategy that I use very successfully with clients is illustrated in the diagram on the next page. It explains how our bodies and brains process our thoughts and how we create pain or pleasure for ourselves as a result of what we think. Look at this diagram whenever anything happens in your life that results in your experiencing a physical and emotional reaction. It's part of the toolkit I use with all my clients, and I know you will find it invaluable. So let me explain how it works.

As I have said before, in a divorce or separation many unexpected or even expected things are happening on a daily basis. From the email telling you that your ex will be late to pick up the kids, to the post that arrives with yet another bill to pay, the message from your lawyer that your ex is making some unreasonable demand or the flat tyre that happens on the way to the extra work you are doing to supplement your dwindling funds, if this 'something' that happens is perceived as having a negative impact on you, you will react. Here's how the process works:

1. Bring to mind something quite 'uncomfortable' that happened very recently, perhaps today, yesterday or last week.

The 'What Happened' Diagram

What Happened

She phoned to say she wants to take the children to Australia

$\rightarrow$

Impact Emotion

¥ Stomach tenses

¥ Mouth goes dry

¥ My emotion is:
Fear
Panic

$\rightarrow$

What I Make It Mean

¥ I'll lose my kids.

¥ It's all my fault.

¥ I'm a failure.

¥ My kids will forget me.

¥ How will I live without them?

= Stress and pain

$\downarrow$

The quality of the conversations I have in my head defines the quality of my life on a moment-to moment basis. (It also defines the reaction I communicate).

$\rightarrow$

I Need To Separate What Happens From What I Make It Mean Negatively About Me And Ask Myself What Else Could It Mean?

¥ That it is an empty threat to negotiate a better financial deal.

¥ That my kids will grow up in a great environment.

¥ I could move to Australia with them like I've always wanted to.

$\rightarrow$

When It's Impossible for Me to Change the Situation

I must accept the things I cannot control and plan to reduce the negative impact on myself by changing what I make it mean.

2. When it happened, the impact of whatever it was created an immediate reaction which you experienced physically as well as emotionally. Recall the feeling. Where did you experience it in your body? Some people feel it as a sharp pain or perhaps breathlessness in their chests, others as a lurch in their stomachs and others in their necks or shoulders. Where do you experience it and what does it feel like?

3. Once you know where you react in your body, you have just located what we talked about in Chapter 1: your *personal alarm system*. Our bodies are incredibly clever and able to warn us of all kinds of threats and dangers. This reaction is called the fight-or-flight response and it's produced in our bodies by adrenaline. The physical feelings like a change in breathing, racing heart rate, shaking or an energy surge are the products of a physical response to an emotional situation. Our minds and bodies are so interconnected that it's virtually impossible to experience an emotion without a physical reaction.

4. Give your physical reaction a name or a label. It could be something like 'winded' or 'a gut feeling' or 'tenseness' or 'a shiver'. From my experience I have found that most people have exactly the same physical reaction whenever they experience a threatening or confrontational situation. For me I always react with tenseness in my chest and generally pull at my neck as I move into my emotional thoughts.

5. Next there is the emotion itself. This comes from the thoughts that are beginning to form themselves in your mind. Even before the thoughts have properly articulated themselves, it's possible to name the feelings that arise. Feelings like 'fear', 'panic', 'shock', 'surprise', 'sadness' or whatever it is for you. So go back to the 'what happened'

and now give your emotional thought a label. Whatever comes to mind first is usually exactly right.

6. Now it gets interesting, because what happens next is that once we have the emotional thought in place, we move swiftly across into the 'meaning' area of the diagram and add some, usually negative, meanings to the emotional thought.

7. So what do you make the 'what happened' mean negatively about you? Take your own example. What did you make it mean? Was it something like, 'I won't have enough money,' 'I won't be able to parent my kids properly,' 'I'm never going to be loved again,' 'I can't do this by myself,' 'No one understands,' 'I have to do everything'? Create a list of at least five negative meanings.

8. Read through your negative meanings list. A typical list might look like:

- I am a failing as a parent.
- My kids will love their other parent more than me.
- I never get what I want.
- I won't have enough money.
- I'll never be happy again.
- I won't get my own needs met.

9. Make your own list and then ask yourself how you are feeling physically and mentally by the time you have experienced your list of negative thoughts. Most people say they feel drained or exhausted, or worse.

10. Look at the fourth box in the diagram. What it's saying is that your negative thoughts define the quality of your life. I know clients

who can take one innocuous occurrence such as a letter that arrives, feel physically sick just because it's in a brown envelope, begin to experience fear and panic off the Richter scale, and make it mean so many negative things that the quality of their life is affected for several days until they finally decide to open the envelope. All that actually happened in reality was that a letter arrived. What they made it mean, and the grief they carried around for such a long time, was actually far worse than the contents of the envelope. So what else could they have done?

11. What else could this mean? What I am asking you to try on for size is the possibility that the 'what happened' doesn't necessarily mean what you *think* it means. Contained in the brown envelope could have been any number of items, and even if it was from your ex's lawyer it doesn't necessarily mean that you will be impacted so negatively that you will be helpless to do anything about it. Virtually every situation and circumstance you will experience during your divorce has a solution of one kind or another that will accommodate you in some way. How do I know? Because the majority of people in the world who divorce go on to lead happy, healthy, fulfilling lives. You will, too. And you can get there with much less stress if you can only separate what happens from what you make it mean. Find another meaning. Opening the letter may mean that you receive vital information that lets you know exactly what your next steps should be. Opening the letter may reveal that your ex has agreed to one of your requests. Opening the letter could even mean that the secretary has forgotten to put the letter in the envelope! This happened to a client of mine who had waited till our call (10 days after receiving the letter) to open it and found nothing

inside! Notice how your thoughts can rule your life if you let them. With this awareness, you realize you always have a choice regarding your reaction and response.

12. Lastly, there are things that happen that you simply cannot do anything about: the flat tyre on the way to pick up the kids from school, the beautiful picture frame that you treasured that gets blown off the window sill and breaks, the rain on the day you had planned a picnic. Once again, the only option you have is to *change what you make it mean*. By phoning your friend to pick up your kids you realize that sometimes you just need to ask for help and people are happy to support you. Your broken photo frame wakes you up to the people who are so precious in your life, so you call them up or do something special for them. The rain means you can choose a creative alternative by staying in and playing with your kids after a sandwich lunch on a rug on the floor. Sometimes we have to go with the flow, change our thoughts and change our rigid control of our lives as a consequence.

Be Resourceful, Not Resistant

The truth is that your pain and upset are not caused by 'what happened'. Your pain and upset are caused by *your thoughts*, which keep you resisting and fighting against what happened. When you are able to let go of your resistance, in fact even be *willing* for anything to happen, the need to fight and resist simply disappears.

Being willing for anything to happen doesn't mean you become passive or allow the world to take advantage of you. Of course you will act in a way that ensures your safety and stability. But being willing means that, whatever happens, you have the ability to change your thoughts and change what you are making things mean. Letting go of resistance allows you to be constructive and take the appropriate actions needed to do whatever you have to to address any and all situations and circumstances that present themselves to you.

Learning to Trust Yourself

Learn to trust that you will be OK, that you will be fine, in fact you will be even better as a result of learning how to be creative and resourceful in any given situation. Build up some evidence. Every time you survive a situation that arises, from mildly threatening in some way to what feels like a major threat, make a note of what you did in order to handle the situation. Put it in your Divorce Diary under 'Evidence that I Can Trust Myself'. The more evidence you acquire that you can trust yourself to handle each and every situation, the more confident you will be that you can take back control of your life. Letting go and knowing you can trust yourself to take care of business without fear is the key to self-responsibility and your ultimate peace of mind.

If you use the 'what happened' diagram whenever something evokes an emotional reaction, you will be able to change the way you react to everything that happens in your life and find new, improved solutions that will inspire and empower you as you take control of your everyday life.

Next Steps

After this thorough inspection of your ego mind, it's time to go one step further. My intention is that you get to the bottom of all your hurts and upset so that you can choose the way you live rather than just taking whatever life throws at you. For this we need to delve into the subconscious mind.

The Subconscious Mind

The subconscious mind is connected to the ego mind, but you have to dig a little deeper to access it. This is the mind that knows everything about you and understands that there is a time and purpose for everything that happens to you. It's the mind that doesn't judge, doesn't make a drama out of anything. It's the pure aware mind. It doesn't deny that you are in pain; it allows you to feel pain in all its intensity, understand it, learn from it, accept it and go beyond it. The subconscious mind is like listening to your soul and having a conversation with the place inside you that holds the truth about everything. It's your inner knowing.

The ego mind, with all that it has made up about your life, with its saboteur and alerter, can keep you in fear and panic. The subconscious mind will lead you to peace.

Because the ego mind is made up of all the thoughts and beliefs about life that we have acquired along the way, it has strong references to draw on. When your ego mind meets up with another's, namely your ex's, each one will try hard to make the other fit into its beliefs about what relationships should be like. It's inevitable that eventually you'll run into difficulties. It may be hard to believe, but your partner showed up in answer to a call from your ego mind. You attracted to yourself exactly the kind of person you needed in order to learn more about yourself and who you are. I say this because, without question, all of my clients report an increased understanding of 'self' after divorce, even if they do have to repeat some of their old patterns to learn the lesson fully. No one gets divorced without experiencing more inner knowledge than they had before.

The most challenging concept is that you are not just your ego mind. That's simply your creation. You have a soul, and if your soul could speak to you and you were able to listen, you would hear the truth about your relationship and the role you have played in it.

Your Ultimate Wake-up Call

The end of your relationship has opened a door to your soul that lets in all the scariest things you could ever think of facing. Now you have to confront your darkest fears and your wildest dreams. You have to listen to your soul. Your subconscious mind has been patiently waiting for you to wake up and surrender to yourself, to tell yourself the truth, to accept, learn, forgive and move on.

The Illusion

The thoughts and beliefs that are part of your old wiring make it seem that the absolute truth is that you needed this other person to complete your life or make you whole. Your thoughts and beliefs make it seem like you owe the other person something; that you need to be responsible for them, that you have to take care of them. You have identified yourself with the ego mind part of you that holds on with a vice-like grip to what it has made up about what you need, or what you must have or what you must do. These thoughts crowd your mind and suffocate your true nature.

It's an illusion. Why does the ego do this? Well, just imagine if you didn't have your stories about being lonely, having less money, being loved again, having status or a role, being looked after, being able to care for yourself or having to take care of someone else. Imagine if you were not concerned about how your partner would manage without you, that you had failed or let them down or that they had done the same to you, that you had misled them and hurt them, or they you. Who would you be? What kind of person would you be if you didn't have any of those feelings?

You tell me. Would you be a vile, irresponsible, disconnected, isolated, uncaring person? If you think that, you have stepped right back in the ego mind, making up something about everything and remaining stuck and in pain.

I'm not saying that you shouldn't have these feelings, and I know that anyone would agree that they are perfectly justified. All I am saying is that it's possible that these feelings and beliefs are not the absolute truth, and that you are confusing everything you have believed in the past about how your partner is and how your life is with them, with what's really true for you deep in your soul. From this ego mind perspective you stay stuck one foot in and one foot out of your relationship.

Emotionally divorcing from your ex means accepting what you cannot change and letting go of all your old painful stories that keep you emotionally attached.

Emotionally divorcing is letting go of the ego-controlled mind about the way 'it is' and moving into a place of conscious acceptance of the pain of loss, experiencing that pain, giving it your fullest attention, understanding it, learning from it. Only in that way can you return to the peaceful place that lives in your soul, which is a place of ease and knowing. So how you can you do that?

The Challenge

The challenge for you is to live with both your ego mind and your subconscious mind at the same time, and blend the two together into a practical everyday way of living. Your job is to be open to listening to your subconscious mind so that your ego mind has moments of respite from its constant chatter and haranguing. That's what meditation is all about. It's about giving your ego mind a rest so that you can listen to your inner self. It's about listening to the part of you that understands the truth about what is happening and knows, deep down, that it is all for your higher good in the end.

Back to Emily and Tom's Story
Before I show you the exercise, let's return to Emily and Tom. As it turned out, Tom received some help from the NHS and a charity set up to help parents with MS. Emily moved out with George and Casey and took the children to see Tom each week. The children learned how to understand their dad's illness and this added another dimension to their young lives. It was a long journey for Emily, but I helped her learn how to live with her guilt and her liberation, holding both in her heart as valid parts of herself.

By practising the following exercise, Emily was able to accept that we are all made up of both dark and light, and she learned to *embrace all her feelings as equal and let them live side by side in her heart*.

You can help yourself accept this, too.

The Open Heart Strategy
This is a tried-and-tested strategy for blending the ego mind and the subconscious mind together. I suggest you first read it through from beginning to end. As you read it through, you may experience some resistance. Just notice any resistance and keep reading through to the end. Put your judgements on hold and put the strategy to work.

Find a comfortable place to sit or lie down. Bring your attention to your breath. Begin to breathe in and out, focusing on the rise and fall of your tummy as you inhale and exhale. Let your body relax. As you breathe in, notice which parts of you are tense. Breathe into

The Ex Files | 101

these areas of your body and, as you exhale, release the tenseness and let go. Breathe into each and every part of your body where you feel tenseness, and each time you exhale you are able to relax even more deeply.

Now turn your attention to a time in your life when you unintentionally upset someone, made a small error of judgement or made a mistake, but you were able to resolve it. Remember what happened, what you said, what you did, how you felt. See yourself as you were then, hear what you heard and feel what you felt and, as you inhale, take that image of yourself making the mistake, upsetting someone or judging wrongly and place that image of you as you were then into your heart.

Now recall a time in your life when you made a more serious error of judgement, where you accused someone of something that they didn't do, when you made an error that had deeper consequences for you and the other person. Once again, see yourself as you were then, hear what you heard and feel what you felt, and as you inhale take that image of yourself making the mistake, upsetting someone or judging wrongly and place that image of yourself into your heart.

Notice that your heart is able to expand to make room for each upset and each mistake without judging it. You heart will just allow it in and accept it as part of you.

Now think of a time when someone hurt you, upset you and misjudged you and misunderstood you in a way that had negative consequences for you. Begin with your ex-partner. Start with something small that happened. Hear them saying what they said, see them doing what they did. See yourself experiencing the feeling of hurt and upset you felt and recall how much you wanted to push them away from you.

Inhale deeply and breathe into your chest. Take that image of your ex making the mistake, upsetting you or judging you wrongly, and place that image into your heart. Feel your heart expand. Notice that your heart is big enough to contain all your hurts as well as everything and everyone that you love. Inhale into your chest and breathe the misjudgements your ex-partner made about you into your heart. Do not resist, do not push them away.

You may struggle with this exercise, but by trying to put painful experiences out of your heart, somewhere outside yourself, your ego mind sits in judgement of them. Doing the exercise does not mean that you are condoning any unacceptable behaviour. It does not mean you still want to be with your partner. It simply means that you are willing to live with the truth. It means that you are able to accept the ego mind's way of thinking as well as the truth that the subconscious mind is aware of. In this way you allow the truth of your soul to heal the pain of your ego mind by having them live together in your heart.

Next time, repeat this exercise with deeper and even more impactful hurts that are still painful for you right now. Do not resist, do not push them away.

By practising this exercise as often as every day if you need to, breathing in all upsets you attribute to your ex-partner and allowing your subconscious mind to open up to your inner knowing and truth, you will find that it becomes easier to accept what you cannot change. Then, instead of remaining in the drama of blame and upset, your heart will remain open and more peaceful.

Getting Practical – Your Personal Boundaries

Having looked at what's going on inside you, it's time to return to the practical world of taking specific actions that will make a positive difference to your everyday life. In order to move away from the pain of loss and everything else you make your divorce mean, towards that far-off place called 'pleasure', you'll need to be acutely aware of how you handle yourself and how you handle your ex. You'll need to create an attitude which reflects your intention to detach yourself emotionally and physically from this relationship. You'll need to have the right tools in place to allow you to take the actions necessary to put the right kind of personal boundaries in place that keep you safe and sane. You need to know that how you feel about your ex will change over time. You won't always react negatively to their every word or action. Right now, though, your recovery is your priority. So let's begin with …

Living with the Enemy

For many people, the end of a relationship heralds the beginning of one of the most uncomfortable parts of the divorce process – that time when you both know the relationship has ended but you still have to live together in the same house.

How awful to live with someone you don't want to be with. They can't leave because either they don't have the money to move or they are unwell and need to remain at home, or they believe if they drag the process out for as long as possible you may just change your mind and have them back again. For whatever reason, 'living together apart' can be extremely difficult.

Alison and Phil's Story

Alison was 36 when she discovered that Phil had been having a four-year affair with their mutual friend Lorraine. Alison's discovery was brutal and embarrassing. She had been sitting by the swimming pool of the tennis club that she and Phil belonged to one sunny summer day with her friend Angela. Angela's and Alison's children were playing happily in the shallows and the pool terrace was full of mums and happy kids enjoying themselves. In the corner of the terrace an argument erupted between two women. One of the women was Lorraine. Suddenly the other woman got up and marched towards the changing rooms. Noticing Alison look up, she turned on her heel and purposefully marched back. She took up a position right in front of Alison and said very loudly, much to the interest of most of the onlookers, 'And *you* are the biggest idiot of all, Alison, because you don't even know that your husband has been having an affair with Lorraine right under your stupid nose!'

To say that Alison was shocked to the core would be an understatement. She tells me that she simply does not remember getting the kids dressed or driving home. That evening she confronted Phil, who denied it all. Alison moved into that unreal world of 'Am I going crazy?' as her marriage slowly unravelled around her. She remembered the holidays where Lorraine had spent so much time with Phil because they both loved to play table tennis. The times when Lorraine was the one who had rubbed suntan lotion on Phil because, after all, she was a masseuse. She remembered times when Phil had had to 'pop over' to Lorraine's to drop something back for one of the children.

If she'd needed any more proof, it came shortly afterwards. She ran into another friend, Rachel, who owned a local jewellery shop. Just as Alison was about to get into her car, Rachel spotted her and rushed over to see if Alison had liked the bracelet that Phil had bought the day before. Alison had not received a bracelet, it was not her birthday any time soon, and here was even more evidence that something was not right. That night she confronted Phil and he admitted he had bought the bracelet for Lorraine.

The game was finally over. Her marriage had clearly been a sham for many years and, like so many women before her, Alison hadn't placed any importance on the little cues and clues along the way. She had ignored signs of discontent because she simply hadn't realized how important they were. Besides, she had trusted Phil. They had been together for 16 years. Now it was all over.

However, Phil could not move out immediately. Finances meant that Alison ended up sleeping on the sofa for the next ten months – because, after all, Phil had to go to work and she was a stay-at-home mum. The winter of their discontent began.

The overriding feeling that grew like a cancer inside Alison was anger. This was an anger that she had never experienced before. It came through her pores and manifested itself through massive weight loss. It was an unspeakable anger. She could not bear to be anywhere near Phil. She stopped cooking his meals or washing his clothes. She spoke to him as little as possible. The more she withdrew, the more he felt guilty and tried to be as pleasant as he could. For some reason, this made it even worse for Alison and most of their interactions were hysterical, even verging on violent. After one 'slipper throwing' incident a hysterical Alison called the police to have him taken away.

Neither of them had any idea how to manage themselves or their lives during this time. Their home became a battleground where blame, resentment, guilt and sadness fought a war that had no ceasefires. Phil went out as much as he could and Alison stayed home eating herself up with bitterness. By the time Phil left, both of them were completely worn out. When Alison came to see me she was on antidepressants, had bitten her nails to the quick and was painfully thin. It could all have been so much easier if they had only had the resources to deal with their situation.

Living Together Boundaries

If you have to live together while waiting to live apart, you'll need to become aware of your own emotional boundaries. When you know what they are and you put them in place, they will allow you to manage yourself and your emotions on a daily basis.

If you are already living apart, many of the same boundaries still apply and you can select the appropriate guidelines for your specific circumstances.

First, though, you'll need to know what your emotional boundaries are.

Taking your emotional temperature each day is a vital exercise and an indicator of the control you currently have available to make rational decisions. To lower your temperature so that you can control your emotional state on a daily basis, you need to gain an awareness of why it is raised in the first place. This is the time to let your head rule your heart and use your brain instead of your emotions.

In order to begin the letting-go process while still living together, and to create personal boundaries that allow you to regain your individuality and feel safe, you need to be really clear about what you want. Take a look at each of the following points.

- The way you talk and listen to each other
- What needs to be discussed on a daily or weekly basis
- How you will handle the finances
- When money will be paid into the bank account
- What to share in terms of food, household products, cooking, cleaning
- What's your property and what is shared property
- What's your personal space, what is his or hers and what is shared
- How you will parent
- Where you will sleep
- The consequences of overstepping each other's personal boundaries.

The last point – the consequences of overstepping each other's boundaries – is particularly important. In order to have boundaries in the first place you have to be extremely clear about what you will and will not tolerate.

Each of you should know the consequences that will result if either of you crosses the other's boundaries. This is not a veiled threat; this is a prerequisite in boundary setting. If the other person knows what is expected and agrees to the expectations, and they know what will happen if those expectations are not met, as long as you follow through on the consequences, firm boundaries will be established.

This may be the first time you have set personal boundaries with your ex. Setting them will allow you to begin to trust yourself and, to some extent, your ex, and at the same time help you to grow into a person who understands how to create safety for themselves. Without good boundaries in place you are simply inviting an invasion of your personal space, time or property. Without consequences in place you may experience boundary violations such as disrespect or even mental and/or physical abuse. Worst of all, without clear personal boundaries in place you are disrespecting yourself and devaluing your own worth.

House Rules

Sleeping with the Enemy

If you have decided to split up, sleeping in the same bed as your ex is really confusing for both of you. Most women in this situation say something like 'I lie next to him and hear him breathing and I cry. I cry for what we could have had, what we don't have, what I have lost and I feel so many mixed emotions.' Most men say something like, 'I lie next to her and I don't know what to say or do. I'm tired and I don't want to talk, so I just turn over and go to sleep.' Both end up exhausted in the morning.

It's very hard to be this close when you have decided to be apart. The best way round it is for one of to sleep in another room. When space is limited, you will need to be creative about this. If there is simply no way round, at the very least invest in single beds and put a bedside table in between.

Sex with Your Ex

Sex with your ex will mess up your mind. And it can be so very tempting. You know each other intimately and you both know you will receive immediate gratification from each other, and it's been ages – and besides, you just need it. But however powerful your attraction to each other physically, it's important to stay focused on the reasons why you are breaking up. If you are the one who is being left and you have sex with your ex-partner, they will be having their cake and eating it too. If you are the one who is leaving, then you are using your ex for instant gratification and taking advantage of him or her.

Yet another reason not to have sex with your ex is the act itself. Nothing brings you physically, literally, closer to your partner than sex, and it's more than likely that during and after sex strong feelings will resurface. It's very easy to confuse this with love. The hormones that are triggered during sex have the power to make you feel like you are falling in love again. This emotion may evoke memories of good times together and bring on amnesia about the real reasons your relationship has ended. It won't change the problems you have been experiencing but may bring up new ones, especially if you have unprotected sex.

If after all of the above you are still willing to have sex with your ex, maybe there are still some unresolved issues for you both. If you both feel able to be this close, is it possible that with the right kind of intervention from a counsellor or therapist there is a way to resolve your differences? I don't have the answer for you unless I'm working with you, but I do know that even the most fabulous sex is not enough to sustain a relationship when there are other much deeper issues to address.

Dependence

Do you still want to tell your ex the details of your day and act as if you were still a couple? If you are still in the same house, do you want your ex to make certain decisions, eat meals with you and be part of the family? If the answer is yes, you are still emotionally entwined. If your ex is unwilling to co-operate with you in this way, it will be because he or she doesn't want to confuse the situation and emotionally and physically cross boundaries.

It's true that some couples are able to manage courteous conversation, and some couples have an intention to remain friends either for the sake of the children or because they have covered a great deal of emotional ground and worked hard on themselves to create a good working relationship for the future. But if this is not something the two of you have discussed and agreed upon, it's more likely that you are stuck in shock and denial and are finding it difficult to accept the reality of your situation. You may need some support – from friends or a professional – to work through the early emotional stages of the divorce process so that you can gain control over your emotions and begin the journey of acceptance.

Healing Language

The way you and your ex speak to each other should make up a critical part of your agreed boundaries. Over the years I have studied many different ways to help people communicate effectively. Some of the tools I now use are a combination of techniques passed down by parenting expert Dr Thomas Gordon, person-centred therapist Carl Rogers, Co-active coaching models, NLP (neuro-linguistic programming) and authors such as the fabulous Jonathan Robinson and John Gray, all of whom have contributed to the strategies you'll find in this book. In terms of communication, the following is the kind of language which, if you use it with your ex, will promote a healing relationship rather than one fraught with conflict.

This is a structured piece of work, so be prepared to go through the recognized stages of learning with it. At first it will seem contrived and clunky as you consciously formulate your responses in your mind. After a while, though, you will become consciously competent and your responses will feel much more authentic. By the time you have practised this with your ex, your kids, your colleagues, friends, family and even the dog, you will be so unconsciously competent that 90 per cent of your communications will be expressed in the kind of language that promotes respect and the possibility of compassion, understanding and even friendship.

Levels of Listening
The purpose of this technique is to build better relationships through greater understanding. The benefit is that you will gain a greater understanding of what other people are actually saying, instead of making up what you *think* they mean.

Many of us listen to what our partners say (or do) to us and then 'translate' their words or actions into our own language. Our own language is full of assumptions and judgements, and is highly geared towards being over-defensive to protect us from any negative impact.

At this point in time, when your relationship is at its most fragile, it's vital that you understand the power that your thoughts and language will have on the tenuous thread between being able to communicate courteously and decimating the relationship in a single stroke.

The correct time to use this technique is when you have experienced an emotional reaction to something that is said, done or, seemingly, implied.

There are three main levels of listening and here's how they work:

Level 1 Listening

This is about 'what it means to me'. This is where we go into our own interpretation of what the other person has said or done, and begin to 'make up' or assume what they are implying. Generally it's also where we believe there could be a negative impact on us in some way.

This is the ego's sole way of listening. When we listen at Level 1, you can bet our egos are in full bloom. We hear from a place of me, me, me. So what happens is something like this:

Dan says 'I cannot pay for the kid's school trip.'

Jess goes straight into Level 1 Listening and responds with something like:

'That's typical of you. It's OK for you to spend money on your computer and anything else you want. But when it comes to me and the kids, there isn't enough.'

Notice also that Jess's response is based on the track record that Dan seems to have created for himself. It's based on Jess's past experiences of asking Dan for money. Because of this, even if Dan has a valid current reason for not having enough money, Jess is listening from the past and does not have the ears to hear anything new. On top of this there are the assumptions and judgements Jess has made. Jess makes what Dan has said mean that Dan is disrespecting her. Her internal dialogue may sound something like this: 'I know why he doesn't want to give me the money, it's because he has spent it on some other woman. He wants me to feel really bad about myself. I don't even know why I married him. I am making my children suffer as a consequence,' etc., etc.

By the time Jess has run these and more thoughts in her head, her response to Dan destroys the fragile truce they had called.

The good news is that there is another way.

In order not to go into your own head and respond to your ex in the way Jess responded to Dan, you need to be able to listen in a different way.

For one moment, imagine you are from another planet. You have come to Earth understanding how to speak English, but you don't always understand the nuances of it. People are speaking in a tongue you recognize, but you don't understand what they mean simply by what they say. It's like they are talking in code. In order to understand the code you'll need to listen at Level 2, which works like this:

Level 2 Listening

This is about 'what it means to the other person'. At Level 2 you have the opportunity to find out *exactly* what the other person means when they say what they say. This entails:

- **Acknowledging** what the other person has said.

In our example with Jess and Dan, Jess might reflect back to Dan 'You can't pay for the kid's trip?'

All she has done is repeat Dan's words in the form of a question. Instead of going straight into her own translation of what Dan's words mean to her, she is willing to find out what they mean to *him*.

Generally when human beings are asked a question, they dig deep into their databanks and try to find an answer. This means you receive more information. Dan may give Jess an explanation that will lead to a very different conversation.

Don't worry that you'll sound like a parrot. What's interesting about reflecting back exactly what the person has said is that the other person will actually feel heard and acknowledged. Suddenly you are back in rapport with them and on their wavelength. Hearing their own response delivered back to them allows them to think about what they meant by what they've said and hopefully explain it more thoroughly to you.

However, Dan may just respond to Jess's reflection defensively: 'No, I can't.' Now Jess is none the wiser about why Dan can't give her the money, so she needs more information. This entails:

- **Clarification**. For example:
  Jess could say:
  'What do you mean by saying you can't pay for the school trip?' Using 'what' rather than 'why' is important because 'why' is a word that makes people feel they have to defend themselves. Since defence usually comes after an attack, it will immediately feel like you are at war, which is exactly what you don't want.

Dan may now respond by saying 'What I mean is that I can't give you the money for the school trip because I am waiting for my wages to reach the bank. We have had a lot of expenses lately and I am virtually out of funds until next week.'

Now Jess understands why Dan said what he did, she realizes that it had nothing whatsoever to do with what she was making up in her head at Level 1. Using the Level 2 Listening technique avoids accusations, blame and drama. Level 2 Listening is always relationship building while Level 1 is almost always relationship destroying.

The PDQ Method

We all like shortcuts, and there is a time and place for saying what you need to as quickly as possible in certain situations. For example, imagine you are abroad and phoning your ex on your mobile to make a request or inform them of something important. For some reason you can hear that they have misunderstood what you have said by their response. A 'pretty damn quick' way of getting the conversation back on track is to just say 'What did you think I meant by that?' This phrase is a laser- sharp question that addresses the misunderstanding immediately. As we now know, misunderstandings happen at Level 1, so this gives the other person the opportunity to tell you their translation of what you just said, so you can put them straight. This is done without any sarcastic comments such as 'If you learned to listen without jumping down my throat …'.

Any situation that has the potential to be relationship destroying can be pulled back from the brink in a flash with this method. While this method works well in certain situations, though, it's not as powerful a relationship builder as Level 2 Listening with its acknowledgement and clarification, so it should be used with care.

Speaking So Your Spouse Will Listen

Now that you have thoroughly listened to your ex, decoded their message and heard what they were really trying to say to you, you may wish to respond. You may want to let them know the impact their behaviour has on you and help them understand how to get the best out of you if there is to be respect between you.

In order to do this there is a great technique that I have been using for many years in my practice. It's called the four-part message. The four-part message reminds people to communicate what they are feeling and what they want without blame or drama. And it goes like this:

1. 'When you ...' [state the behaviour you want to address, describing – in brief – the *specific* situation. Do not generalize or use words like 'you always', 'you never'. If you do this the other person will immediately go on the defensive.]
2. 'I feel ...' [state the emotion, e.g. sad, hurt, afraid or impatient]
3. 'Because ...' [the impact on you]
4. 'What I want is ...' [describe the *precise* action that you would like your partner to perform (your desired outcome)]

Let's take a look at this in practice:

Old, blameful way of talking: 'You never listen to me.'

Four-part message:

1. 'When you interrupt me when I am speaking, [**specific behaviour**]
2. 'I feel hurt, [your **emotion**]
3. 'Because I believe you are not interested in what I have to say, [**impact on you**]

4. 'What I want is for you to listen to me without interrupting me when I speak so I can properly express myself and then you can give me your response' [**your desired outcome**]

The first part of this message specifies the exact behaviour *without generalizing*, so that the person you are speaking to can tune in immediately to what you are saying. If you generalize or accuse, I can promise you that what you are saying will fall on deaf ears.

The second part of the message is about your feelings. Notice it starts with, 'I feel'. It does *not* say 'You make me feel'. ***No one can make you feel anything.***

The third part of the message addresses the effect their behaviour has on you. This is the 'sales' part of your message. In order for them to 'buy' that their behaviour is not acceptable, you need a great 'selling point'. For example, if I am standing behind you in the supermarket queue and I have seven items in my basket and you have seven items in your basket and I tap you on the shoulder and ask, 'Excuse me, can I go in front of you?', how might you respond? Would you look at me a little askance and wonder why I think I should be entitled to go in front of you? Probably. However, if I tap you on the shoulder and say, 'Excuse me, can I go in front of you because I'm running late and have to pick my son up from school?', chances are you would say 'Go ahead.' I have given you a good enough 'because'.

The fourth part explains what you want the other person to do instead of the behaviour they've originally manifested. We don't always get our desired outcome in life, but if we don't ask for it we never will.

Which part is the most important part of the message? It's the fourth part. Without this part of the message, all the other person hears is your complaint about them without any indication of how to change their behaviour. Your desired outcome gives the other person the opportunity to agree or negotiate new terms with you. It allows you to put your boundaries in place and both of you to know what the other needs without feeling bullied, manipulated or controlled in any way.

Personal Prescription for Managing Your Ex: Five-Day Elimination Process

You are required to get your ex into perspective. He or she is not the enemy and you are not at war. Your task is to eliminate any thoughts that cause you stress of any kind.

Directions for Use

I hope that you will be able to use the skills and strategies contained in this chapter to allow you to move forward in emotionally divorcing your ex and creating a new way of communicating that maintains your dignity and keeps you both from kicking and screaming your way through the divorce courts.

Once again, please be sure to take the full course of medicine I have prescribed for you. You will need to be properly immunized against mismanaging your ex before we begin the next chapter.

Dosage

Each day for the next five days:

- Take your emotional temperature every time you feel an emotional hit and ask yourself the accompanying questions (see page 16).
- Use your 'what happened' diagram to help you work through your upset.
- Gather evidence each day that you can trust yourself to handle whatever situations arise and keep a note of each new triumph in your Divorce Diary.

Self-affirmation Medicine

The following affirmations must be repeated three times each three times a day for five consecutive days.

- Today I will find more evidence that I can handle it.
- Today I will speak without blame and anger.
- Today I will accept what I cannot change and change what I can.

Chapter 5
Kids Don't Divorce

Awareness	Of the emotional impact divorce has on children and families
Attitude	Choosing how you will handle any and all situations that arise
Action	Deciding what actions to take that will best support them

It's just my opinion, but as far as I am concerned if there are children involved in your divorce, they come first. No pressure intended, but I know from speaking to hundreds of parents and from what I've experienced in my own life that how you cope with your kids' reactions and emotions at this sensitive time will shape their lives for the future.

I realize you have your own emotions to cope with, but when there are children involved you come second. Don't take my word for it, though. Visit any family mediator, your own lawyer or ask any court official. When there are kids involved in a relationship break-up, they are always the first priority.

This is where you put yourself and your personal upset on pause for a chapter so we can concentrate on the kids and I can tell you about many of the challenges ahead and what you can do to overcome them.

The Statistics

One in four children in this country lives in a split family. That means that virtually every child in the UK will grow up knowing someone whose parents are divorced. It's vital that we address the consequences that divorce leaves in its wake so we can raise well-balanced kids who understand that even though their parents' relationship didn't work out, it is possible that their parents will learn to heal their hearts, maintain their dignity and go on to love again.

It's vitally important to remember that kids don't divorce, parents do. Divorce is an adult business and whatever you are feeling right now, however challenging your life is, it's just as confusing and challenging for your kids. So it's without question your responsibility to make your divorce as easy as possible for your children. I know that you know this, but I also know that at a time when you are feeling like you need looking after, it's not always easy to focus on their needs first. And you must. You are the adult here. A four-year-old will not be able to cope with a crying mummy when the child is worried about where the puppy will live when Daddy moves out. If you need to cry, find somewhere else to shed your tears away from your kids. I know I am being harsh, but please bear this very much in mind at all times.

Your Child's World
When Kahlil Gibran wrote 'The Prophet', his words hit home for so many parents:

Your children are not your children.
They are the sons and daughters of Life's longing for itself.
They come through you but not from you.
And though they are with you, yet they belong not to you.
You may give them your love but not your thoughts,
For they have their own thoughts.
You may house their bodies but not their souls,

For their souls dwell in the house of tomorrow,
which you cannot visit, not even in your dreams.
You may strive to be like them, but seek not to make them like you.
For life goes not backward nor tarries with yesterday.
You are the bows from which your children as living arrows
are sent forth.
The archer sees the mark upon the path of the infinite, and He bends
you with His might that His arrows may go swift and far.
Let your bending in the archer's hand be for gladness;
For even as He loves the arrow that flies, so He loves also the
bow that is stable.

Gibran goes on to speak about the archer. The archer in the verse is whoever and whatever your God may be. Your children are his 'living arrows'. The archer loves the arrows but he also loves the bow (which is you). And therein lies the essence of this chapter.

The Stable Bow

Your children will, without a doubt, be affected by your divorce. Anything and everything that happens in our lives has an impact on us, and divorce is up there with the most life-changing of them all. You and your partner have been like bookends supporting your children in the middle. Even though you are no longer together you still have to take care of those children and keep them from falling down.

The reality is that you are creating uncertainty where there was once stability. How you handle this will have an impact on the way your children think, feel and act. There is little point assuming that children are resilient and that of course they will survive. While children don't die from divorce, survival by itself is not good enough. Your children have thoughts and feelings of their own. You cannot assume how they will react to your divorce or what they are thinking. Your job, right now, is to step out of your shoes and put yourself in theirs. Then you find out what they need, which may be very different from what you think they need.

What Children Need

Children of different ages will react differently, of course. We'll look at this in more detail, but there is a similarity for all children still living at home.

I asked my own children, who experienced my divorce when they were five and eight (they are now 19 and 22) what they think children need. Here's what they said:

- To feel safe
- To have a happy and stable home to live in
- To be understood and listened to by their parents
- To be loved by both their parents
- To spend quality time with their parents
- To have a routine
- To have friends
- For their parents not to argue with each other
- To be able to pursue activities they enjoy.

This might not be a comprehensive list, but it comes directly from the 'horse's mouth'. You may be able to think of some additions of your own, and I hope you can. Raising your own awareness of what your children need can and will contribute to their healthy emotional development into adulthood.

What Happens When these Needs Are Not Met?

When the needs of your children are not met you can expect consequences in the form of insecurities. These insecurities may lead to a variety of issues. Let's take a look at a few of these.

Children Who Just Tune out and Turn off

If you are emotionally and physically unavailable, your children may retreat to their own inner worlds. If you are not there for them they will learn to avoid you and disconnect from you. As adults they may find relationships difficult and become emotionally and physically distant from their partners.

Children Who Cannot Trust

If you are inconsistent with your children – for example if you are available sometimes and rejecting at others – your children will not know what to expect. This lack of trust in the consistency of your reactions may lead them to behave the same way in their own relationships into adulthood. I have often heard adult clients complain that their partners (current or ex) are either full on with their attention or they withdraw completely. It's very challenging to be in a relationship with someone who acts this way.

Children Who Are Aggressive, Disorganized, Angry and Chaotic

If your children feel ignored or scared to approach you, and their need for emotional closeness is not recognized by you, as they grow into adults they may not be able to give love and affection easily, and may be insensitive and unresponsive to their partner's needs.

Children Who Experience Developmental Difficulties

As a result of detachment between you and your children, it's possible that they may experience mental or physical health problems, learning difficulties and/or an inability to create good social skills.

Often children manifest reactions in several of these areas. This has nothing to do with socio-economic or cultural differences. These reactions are similar in most children who are not getting their primary needs met.

Other Causes of Children's Insecurity

- Physical neglect – as in cases where children's basic needs for nutrition and medical attention go unmet
- Emotional neglect or abuse
- Physical or sexual abuse
- Separation from the primary carer – as a result of circumstances such as death, illness, divorce or being taken into care
- Constantly changing environments
- Parental depression
- Parental drug or alcohol abuse
- Lack of parenting skills

It's vital to understand that our children experience their first 'love' relationships with their parents. Learning how to love and be loved begins at birth, and as parents we have the power to shape and influence our children's experience of love. Therefore it's vitally important that we are committed to behaving in a way that allows our children to experience the sheer joy of being loved and learning how to love in return.

Tuning back in

In order to create the right environment for your children to grow emotionally, you only need look back to the time when they were born. They could not speak but most of the time you were able to tune in to their needs. You looked at them, you picked them up, you fed them and changed them and they didn't have to say a word. You tuned in to their need and were able to provide it for them.

Stepping into My Child's World

- In your mind, take a physical and emotional step back from your situation. In your mind's eye, imagine your child standing in front of you. You can see from the top of their head right down to their shoes. Observe them. See what they look like, how they stand and the expression on their face. Ask yourself, 'What does my child need right now?' Take a moment to hear the answer. This is what *you* think your child needs.

- Now in your mind, move out of your body and transport yourself into your child's body.

- What does it feel like being in your child's body?
  What emotions are you experiencing? What are your fears, your concerns? What's going on for you?

- Now, whilst being your child, ask yourself, 'What do I need?' Take your time and listen for the answer.

- Move back into your own body and observe your child. Now what do you see? What do you experience when you look at your child? How do you respond? What's needed? Do they need to be hugged, played with or listened to? Do they need to be acknowledged and then given some privacy?

> Do they want time with you? What do they need that they
> are expressing through their behaviours?
> - Go with your intuition. Give them what they need and
>   experience what happens.

If you get it wrong, not to worry, your children will tell you. In most cases, even if they protest, your intuition – especially after practising standing in their shoes – is right. But don't argue. Be guided by them. The fact that you were willing to step into their world and see it through their eyes will reconnect you with your child. They will know that you are trying, and your relationship with them will improve as a result.

Staying Together for the Sake of the Children

One of the questions you might still be asking yourself is if you should stay in your marriage for the sake of the kids. Personally I do not advocate remaining in an unhappy relationship and sacrificing your soul for the sake of your kids, even though I know that yours are pretty special. However, if there is the slightest chance that you could revive your relationship, make it work between you and rebuild a happy family life, obviously that's the most ideal situation for your children. But in cases where life has become intolerable and your home has become a war zone, your kids will suffer anyway. We all know couples who have stayed together for the duration of their children's upbringing and put their own lives on the back burner, but this brings its own sorrows.

Linda and Jeffrey had been married for 25 years. When Jeffrey asked Linda for a divorce, he was surprised at her reaction. Their girls, aged 23 and 25, had completed their studies, left home and were both able to support themselves. Jeffrey told me he had been waiting for this moment, when all his responsibilities would be at an end and he would finally be free. He had been unhappy with Linda for the previous 15 years. He was sure she knew this. However, he never would have contemplated leaving the kids and he thought that this was some kind of unspoken agreement between them.

When they met, Linda was 19 and Jeffrey was 20. He had never really intended to have a long-term relationship with her, but Linda had fallen pregnant and, as Jeffrey had been adopted at five years old, asking Linda to give up their child was simply not an option for him. He did the honourable thing and married her. Linda had been brought up in a Catholic home and was very grateful that Jeffrey was so responsible.

It had become quite clear in the first year that they had little in common. They liked different food, different TV programmes, different music. All they had in common was the fact that they both adored their daughter. None of this really bothered Linda in the early stages of being a mother. She was so busy she didn't even notice. Now they had a child Jeffrey had no intention of leaving Linda, so when she proposed that they had a second child he did not object. He had already decided he was in it 'for the long haul'. They created a family unit that worked well as long as they put the children first. While the children were growing up they rubbed along together quite well. It wasn't as if they argued; they just didn't spend much time alone together. Life chugged along and Jeffrey began to participate in all kinds of sporting activities. Linda learned to paint and she ran meditation classes for women.

Linda was genuinely happy with her lot, and had thought that Jeffrey was, too. As the girls grew up and family outings and holidays changed accordingly, their children needed them less. This meant that the time Jeffrey and Linda spent together decreased accordingly.

To Jeffrey's complete surprise, Linda was incredibly angry when he announced his desire to divorce. Why had he waited so long to tell her his real feelings? She had thought that they had a way of being together that worked. She had accepted that, while there were no fireworks in their relationship, there were no battles either. She had enjoyed the freedom of pursuing her projects and was happy for Jeffrey to have his freedom too. Jeffrey, however, had misguidedly thought that Linda felt the same way he did. After all, their sex life was non-existent and they even cooked for themselves now as their tastes were so different. He was honestly surprised at her reaction. Didn't she realize that the only reason he'd stayed so long was that he'd wanted to be a good father? Linda responded by saying didn't he realize that he had stolen the best years of her life?

When the girls were told by their sobbing mother about their father's announcement, they were stunned and very angry. While he had provided so much for them in every way, to do it at the expense of his own and their mother's happiness made them feel incredibly guilty. On top of this, it seemed as if their whole perception of their upbringing was now in question. Was any of it real? At 23 and 25, they could no longer use the model of their parents' marriage as a template in their own relationships. They now had to consider their own behaviour and their own prospects of having happy, healthy relationships.

Staying together for the sake of your children is not always best. Children inevitably grow up and leave home, and it's not always easy to dust yourself down and pick up the pieces when you're older.

If it sounds like you are caught between the devil and the deep blue sea, damned if you do leave and damned if you don't, I'd like to point out that it's not all doom and gloom. Children are not necessarily scarred for life when their parents split up, as long as the parenting from Mum and Dad continues to be great and attentive, and their parents can maintain civility and not draw their children into their own battles. If you can manage that, it's totally possible to raise well-balanced children who grow into loving, compassionate adults.

What Do We Tell the Kids?

While this will depend on the ages of your children, bearing in mind the 'needs' listed earlier, *all* children will need reassurance of some kind or other.

Children Aged 2½–8

Planning ahead is vital, as is timing. This is not something that should be announced in anger, when you're upset or because you want to tell them 'exactly what kind of a mother (or father) they have' (not unless you want to engrave an indelible memory of the worst day of their lives in their young minds!). I suggest that, if possible, you *and* your partner tell your children together in the same room. Ideally, it needs to be done during the day, when you can go on to do something else all *together* afterwards. Remember, this is not about you! Both of you should be available after the announcement and be prepared for any questions that could arise.

Imagine you choose a Saturday morning. After breakfast you might go into your sitting room and ask the kids to come in because you want to speak to them. If they are young, put them on your laps or sit them together opposite you or where you can look at them directly. I suggest you sit next to your partner, but keep the kids close, not on the other side of the room.

You need to keep it very simple. Divorce is an adult business. Children are only looking for reassurance that life as they know it will not fall apart. They really don't need to know who betrayed whom. That's too much information.

The conversation might go something like this:

'Mummy and Daddy have decided that we are not going to be married any more and we are going to be just friends instead.' *Pause here and wait for any specific reactions. There may be questions at this point, generally about what this statement means. They will already be trying to work out what this means to them.*

'This means that Daddy is going to live in another house and you will stay here with Mummy. You will see Daddy very often. We both love you very, very much and this is between Mummy and Daddy and it's a grown-up thing.'

It's impossible to tell what they've understood and what's going on in their minds at this point. So don't assume. One mother told me that after they had broken the news to their children, her son, aged four, burst into tears. Both of them thought it was because the news was such a shock. They let him cry for a bit and cuddled him. Mum went back into the 'We love you very much' part when their son said, 'Yes, I know that, but what I want to know is who is going to get the fridge magnets?'

The world looks very different through your children's eyes. Never assume you know what they are thinking or feeling. The only way of finding out is to ask.

After your announcement, be prepared for the questions. One of the first you can expect is: 'Are you getting divorced?'

From five upwards, your children probably already know friends with divorced parents, or have heard the word at school or on TV. However, what they make up in their heads is not cut and dried. You need to find out what 'divorce' means to them so you can reassure them further. This takes a very special kind of listening.

So, you might respond, 'Yes, we will one day, but I'm wondering what you think getting divorced means?'

Your child may refer to someone he knows and say something like, 'Daddy goes away and doesn't come back.'

Reflect back so your child feels acknowledged and heard: 'So you think Daddy may go away and not come back?'

'Yes.'

'Well, Daddy will go and live somewhere else, but he will see you every weekend (or whatever your arrangements are) and you'll be able to speak to him every day on the telephone. Daddy loves you very much and he will always be there for you. He is not going to leave you. Is there anything else that is worrying you?'

Be prepared to hear more and then go through the process again.

The reassurance is in the listening. When a child is listened to and acknowledged, he feels safe enough to ask further questions. If you fob him off with anything other than the simple truth, he will eventually close down because he won't be able to trust that you understand what's going on for him. Young children find it hard to get their heads round this situation. Many find it difficult to articulate these new feelings. That's not surprising, because they have never had them before. Life has been predictable and certain. Now it's not. You'll need patience and compassion, and then more patience. Listen first, and then answer simply and honestly.

'Why don't you want to be married any more?' This is quite a sophisticated question for young ones but it comes up, along with variations like, 'Don't you love each other any more?'

In response, you can say, 'Well, Mummy and I still care about each other (even if you don't!) but we have decided that we prefer to be friends. We both love you very much and that will never change.'

Another thought that plays on kids' minds is, 'If you don't love each other any more, then one day you might stop loving me.' It makes sense, doesn't it? The simple answer is, 'It's impossible for mummies and daddies to stop loving their children, so you don't have to worry.'

Kids Behaving Badly?

Most young children don't ask too many questions, but their behaviour changes. They don't want to go to bed or they start playing up after coming home from seeing Mum or Dad. They have tantrums, shout and scream and they climb into bed with you when they'd been sleeping so well in their own beds. They revert to wetting at night or wetting during the day. There is such a variety of scenarios that you could write a whole book just describing them. Your job is to be aware. This is not bad behaviour. It's just behaviour.

For example, if your child plays up before bedtime, acknowledge what is going on rather than letting your tiredness and frustration out. It could very well be that they are missing their other parent and simply cannot articulate it. Say, 'You really don't want to go to bed, do you?'

'No.'

'I understand, but it is bedtime now. Would you like to speak to Daddy on the phone before you go to bed?'

Mostly they will say yes, and so you ring your ex and tell them that Amy would like to say goodnight and have a kiss down the phone. Nine times out of ten this works well. Amy feels safe and reassured and will go to bed. Yes, it may become a habit and sometimes Daddy may not be available. So be creative. Have a recorded message to play when Daddy isn't available, or get your child to leave him a goodnight message on his answerphone. You may arrange with your partner to call at a certain time. This is for you to work out. Once your child feels safe and reassured, she won't need this all the time.

If they have tantrums, try to hold them still with your arms around them and reassure them that they are safe. Ask them if they feel sad or scared, and what the 'tantrum' wants to say. Try to get them to speak about their feelings. This will be hard for them to articulate but use simple language.

For sure there will be a bit of attention seeking and maybe even some playing off of you against your ex. For example, 'Daddy lets me get into his bed, so why don't you?' In this instance, find the right time during the day, when all is calm, and explain what your needs are. Then ask them what they would need in their bedrooms when they wake up if they cannot come into your bed. One mother tried this with her three-year-old and he said he needed to take off his wet nappy. His mother showed him how to pull off his wet night-nappy pants, put them in a carrier bag and put a fresh pair on. He then said he got thirsty and would need a drink, which she provided in a spill-proof beaker. They also arranged his 'Daddy teddy' to be sitting in a certain place so he could see it when he woke up. Anticipate your child's needs; prepare as much as possible, and set boundaries that you stick to.

Children Aged 9–12

Children in this age group are far more aware. They may have a good idea of why you are breaking up. They may be embarrassed about it and not want to talk about it. It's all terribly uncomfortable. The older they are, the more of an impact your behaviour may already have had on them over the previous months or even years. They are still young, so although they are more articulate and can make more sense of it all, they are still powerless to do anything about it.

Some children in this age bracket will become repressed and their behaviour at school may change. They may pay less attention, underachieve or develop ailments such as headaches or stomach aches.

Their bodies are swallowing up their pain. It's vital to get children of this age to talk. Take your cues and clues from them.

My own daughter was a point in case, and she has kindly given me permission to tell her story.

A few months after we divorced, when Carly had just turned nine, I had arranged to meet her at school for Book Day. I was to bring her little brightly coloured beaded purse with her pocket money in it, so she could buy herself a book. I went to her room to get the purse and was really surprised at how heavy it was. When I opened it I was totally shocked. There were pound coins, £5 notes, £10 notes and even a £20 note. I couldn't understand it. I went to school with her purse, and when I got there I said to her, 'Carly, I picked up your purse and noticed it contained a great deal of money which I don't think is yours.' She said, 'Yes, it is, yes, it is' and started getting very upset and overwrought. I told her that we wouldn't talk about it just then, but when we got home we would have to sit down and talk together. Carly bought her book and when we got home, much to her discomfort, I took her in the lounge and said we needed to talk. She squirmed and wriggled and would not look at me. So I suggested we turn our backs to each other; I told her, 'Then you won't have to look at me while we are talking.'

So we sat back to back and I said to Carly that there was so much money in the purse that couldn't possibly be hers, as she only got 25p a week pocket money (it was a long time ago!). She insisted the money was hers and that she had 'found it'. She said she needed it because she wanted to be rich. I had no idea what all this was about, so I simply acknowledged her by reflecting back to her, 'You wanted to be rich?' She said 'Yes, because at school some people have got a mummy and daddy who live together and I don't, so if I can't have that, I want to be rich instead.' Then she added, 'And I wasn't going to spend it, I just wanted to know I had it.' Holding back my tears, I said I really understood how hard it must be not to have a mummy and daddy together, but taking money that didn't belong to her was stealing and wrong. 'It's not fair to take money that doesn't belong to you and you can get into a lot of trouble for stealing,' I told her.

It turned out that she had been picking up whatever she could find – either at her dad's place or at home. Whenever either of us had left money out, she'd been gathering it up. I asked, 'But Carly, if I take this money away from you and you are not rich any more, and you don't have Mummy and Daddy living together any more, what will we replace it with?'

It's very upsetting for a child to have something taken away if there's nothing to replace it with. You'll know this if you have small children – take away the fork that they are waving around near their eyes and they'll scream. Replace it with a spoon and you'll have a fairly happy child.

Carly thought about this and said, 'Well, then, I want to have nails like Norma's.' Norma was a mum at the school who had beautifully polished manicured nails. So I suggested that, every Friday, after her bath I would polish her nails for the weekend and she would take it off on Sunday night ready for school. Carly agreed, and that's what we did for the next few weeks until she got bored with it. I also asked her if I could leave money around the house and know that she would not take it. She agreed and we never had another moment's problem with her taking anything that didn't belong to her.

So much to learn. This age group says less and does more. If I had not caught this she could have ended up stealing from the sweetshop, and might even have progressed to bigger things. I understood that Carly was experiencing a loss of identity. Carly was asking herself, 'Who am I and where do I fit in?' This, the most profound and poignant question every human being asks themselves at some point in their lives, was coming from a nine-year-old. Every behaviour your child exhibits will be based on this question. Carly was asking, 'Who am I now that my mummy and daddy are not together?' She found a way of fitting in so she could be 'someone' – someone rich, someone with her own power.

Without our identity intact we can slowly disappear to ourselves. It's the same for our children, whatever their age group. That's why it's so important to spot the signs even when they are not as obvious as Carly's were.

The 9–12 age group needs care and attention. Inform the school of your new living arrangements. Find out if there is a school counsellor, and ask him or her to have an informal chat with your child. Watch your child's behaviour carefully, and listen as if you had three ears. Almost everyone who has been in this situation will have a story to tell. Listen to them all and learn from others who have been through this.

Teenagers

This group comes with a health warning at the best of times, bless them. Every teenager is different, but some are struggling enough with their own hormones and personal identities, and will find it very challenging to add even more change and uncertainty to the mix. Many, on the other hand, will have seen friends go through their parents' divorce and, in general, will be quite resilient and well equipped mentally and emotionally to cope with change.

Telling teenagers is a much more adult affair. I still advocate you tell them together. Say something like,

> 'Mum and I are just not making each other happy any more and we don't want to continue to do this. We have decided it's time to move on with our lives, apart. This is nothing to do with you. This is our doing and we want you to know that we will never stop loving and supporting you. We are always here for you when you need us.'

You can then go on to talk about practical arrangements. Be sure to ask them if they have any questions. Answer them honestly, without blaming your partner, and keep it simple.

As you saw in Linda and Jeffrey's story, older children are more likely to question the relationship itself. How might they have handled it differently? What would they do if they found themselves in a similar situation? Are relationships worth it? There may be questions about sexuality, especially when their parents start dating other people. The thought of one's parents having sex or even going out on a date is pretty 'gross' for most teens. They know you are still capable of this type of behaviour, but as my kids pointed out, there is such a thing as TMI – 'too much information'. Your job is to keep your private life private until such time as it becomes serious enough to warrant talking about.

What Doesn't Work

If you have ever seen any of the Jerry Springer-type talk shows, you will know that there are many people who use their children as pawns in their own game of hurt and revenge towards their partners. If you want to mess up your kids, this is the route you should take.

I never met Michele or Joe because they live in Scotland; however, I do a fair amount of my work by phone. Michele was only 24 but had been married to Joe for three years. They had a two-year-old daughter, Mia. Michele phoned me in a hysterical state and it took some time to calm her down so I could even hear what she had to say. She said Joe had moved out to be with her friend, Kim. Michele was furious. She felt betrayed by Kim and let down by Joe.

Michele decided that she would not allow Joe to see Mia at Kim's house even though he was now living there. She set an ultimatum that Joe could only see Mia for two hours per week, and only if he did not take Mia back to Kim's house. She was determined not to let Mia anywhere near Kim. Putting aside the fact that Joe lived about 15 miles away and didn't have a car, and even though Joe had been a really loving father to Mia, Michele dug in her heels. Battle began, with Mia squarely in the middle.

Of course these stringent visiting arrangements didn't work. Joe would come by bus to pick up Mia, and then would barely have time to take her to the park before he had to get her back to Michele's again. Little Mia didn't understand at all. She was just enjoying being with her daddy and then he was gone. She'd cry and cry for hours after he'd left. She said to Michele, 'Daddy not like me,' which made Michele even more angry with Joe. It simply didn't occur to her that she was helping to make a difficult situation even harder.

It got so bad that Michele decided that Mia was better off not seeing Joe at all, and for the next month Joe was shut out. It was at the end of this month that she called me. Michele knew in her heart that Mia needed to see her daddy, but her anger and hatred towards Kim and her heartbreak over Joe kept her determined not to let Mia anywhere near Kim. What to do?

The first question I asked Michele was, 'Do you want your daughter to have a father?' Of course she said yes. I told Michele that it was absolutely vital that she understood how to manage her own emotions in this sad situation. It was vital, also, that she consider what Mia could possibly be feeling as a result of her daddy's 'disappearance'. Michele was, thankfully, willing to listen and learn.

First we had to get one thing clear: Michele's hurt and anger towards Joe and Kim had absolutely nothing to do with Mia. Michele and Joe once loved each other enough to bring a child into the world, and their parental responsibility remained whether they were together or apart.

You will never be out of your child's life entirely, whether you are with their other parent or not. And, certainly as far as your children are concerned, you will always, always, be the only parents they will ever want.

A Different 'We'

When Michele was married to Joe, she was part of a 'We'. Without Joe, a different kind of 'We' had emerged. Both Joe and Michele became the bookends that support Mia in the middle. She is their 'We'. Forever joined together by their child, and both entitled to be with their child, it's their job to support her so she can grow into a secure, well-adjusted, happy individual.

Nurturing your child through divorce comes before considering your own feelings towards your ex-partner.

The Law of Attachment

British psychiatrist John Bowlby, noted for his expertise in child development, theorized that a child's early experience of social interactions with their parents and other familiar people leads to the development of an 'internal working model of social relationships' – a set of ideas and feelings that establishes a child's expectations about relationships, the behaviour of others towards him and the behaviours appropriate for him towards others.

Your Child's Map of the World

Your child makes sense of the world around her by observing the reactions and responses of her nearest and dearest. Your child is creating her own map of the world, and the decisions she makes about herself and how she is received by others, what is expected of her and what she can expect from others – all of these are being created as she grows. As we mentioned in Chapter 3, the decisions you make about who you are and how life is at an early age will be the story you carry with you for years to come. It will dictate how you react and respond in social situations, it will affect your relationships and, ultimately, it will have tremendous impact on your life.

I know this may all sound a little overwhelming, and as parents we are never going to get it 100 per cent right all of the time, no matter how conscientious we are. We simply have no control over what our children make things mean, or how they experience situations. As Kahlil Gibran said, 'they have their own thoughts.' However, we *can* create as little friction as possible, so that their experience of growing up is as 'normal' as possible.

The Need for Both Parents

In attempting to make your home a sanctuary, and to appreciate the need for your ex's continued presence in your children's lives, let's look at what Bowlby's theories have to offer:

1. *Consistency of care:* 'Feeding and relief of an infant's pain do not cause an infant to become attached to a caregiver. Infants become attached to adults who are sensitive and responsive in social interactions with the infant, and who remain as consistent caregivers for some time.'

2. *Internal working model:* 'Early experiences with caregivers gradually give rise to a system of thoughts, memories, beliefs, expectations, emotions, and behaviors about the self and others. This system ... continues to develop with time and experience and enables the child to handle new types of social interactions.'

3. *Transactional processes:* 'As attachment behaviors change with age, they do so in ways shaped by relationships, not by individual experiences. A child's behavior when reunited with a caregiver after a separation is determined not only by how the caregiver has treated the child before, but on the history of the effects the child has had on the caregiver in the past.'

4. *Consequences of disruption:* 'In spite of the robustness of attachment, significant separation from a familiar caregiver, or frequent changes

of caregiver that prevent development of attachment, may result in psychopathology at some point in later life.'

5. *Developmental changes:* 'Specific attachment behaviors begin with predictable, apparently innate, behavior in infancy, but change with age in ways that are partly determined by experiences and by situational factors. For example, a toddler is likely to cry when separated from his mother, but an eight-year-old is more likely to call out, "When are you coming back to pick me up?" or to turn away and begin the familiar school day.'

The Early Years Are the Most Influential

In studies about how children experience their parents' separation, there is consensus that those who are between the ages of 2½ and 8, whose understanding is necessarily limited, believe that they have in some way *caused* their parents' separation. This age group, therefore, is generally the saddest of all when their parents split up. At 2½, little Mia fits into this category. This is the reason why she is so upset when her daddy leaves. On the plus side, this means that Michele and Joe have already done a very good job in bringing Mia up. However, for Michele to stop Mia's close contact with Joe could have disastrous effects on Mia's sense of wellbeing and security, as well as her ongoing emotional growth.

Developmental psychologist Mary Ainsworth, who built on Bowlby's theories, stated that a child in Mia's situation could develop an 'anxious resistant attachment style'. This plays out in the following way. Her daddy leaves, Mia is distressed. She has only just got reacquainted and he disappears again. If Mia does not see her daddy on a regular basis and for much longer time periods, she may become ambivalent when he does show up. Ainsworth says that 'The mixture of seeking and yet resisting contact and interaction has an unmistakably angry quality, and indeed an angry tone may characterize behavior in the pre-separation episodes.'

This may already be a familiar scenario for you. Your child may want to see her absent parent, yet at the same time resist him when he arrives. It makes total sense. Imagine the scenario. Your most loved person in the world is only available for 120 minutes each week. *You have absolutely no idea why this is.* You go back and forth between longing to see them and being angry that they will disappear again. You have to wait another week (which seems like forever when you are a child), and then the same pattern repeats itself. What do you think a child decides about this? In Mia's words, perhaps 'Daddy not like me.' What do you think she decides about what she can expect from people that she loves? As she gets older, what do you think she decides about *men*, and as a consequence how does she behave around them and how does she value herself with them?

I cannot stress enough what an incredibly powerful position you are in as a parent of a child of divorce. The way you behave now towards your child – and towards the other person who loves them so much (that would be your ex, by the way) – will define your child's life as she develops.

Children's Grief

Children grieve, too. They feel a variety of conflicting emotions just like you do. There will be anger, sadness, hopelessness, powerlessness and disappointment. It hurts and it hurts and it hurts. And that's how they grow. It may take months or even years, depending on the relationship they have with you both and individually. It's a process that takes time, and anything that looks like 'bad behaviour' is only a behaviour that means your child is trying to get his needs met but does not know how to do it any other way.

So how can we help rebuild a family that blooms where it is planted and lives to love another day?

Families that Flourish
Your Parenting Plan
Co-operative parenting is fundamental in ensuring that your kids are able to overcome the impact of divorce, and dictates the kind of relationships they will form in their lives from this point on. I cannot stress enough how important it is to create a parenting plan that works.

A great parenting plan covers the main aspects of caring for your children and creates a win-win situation for the family. Once this is in place and agreed to, a great deal of stress is alleviated for both you and your children. Before I give you some suggestions of how you might do this, I want to explode a myth that many parents want to hold on to when they split up.

The Parenting Myth
From here on in there is no such thing as a 'united front'. It's a fact that, once parents split up, the way they parent their children looks very different to the way they parented when they lived together. While you may still agree on important issues like safety and respect, you may discover that what one parent sees as 'good manners' is not a concern for the other.

When Delia split from Michael, she could not understand why Michael allowed their children (aged 7 and 10) to stay up so late when they stayed with him. They had always agreed that the children needed their sleep in order to function well at school, and now she was hearing that Michael let them stay up to watch 'inappropriate TV' and this meant they were tired the next day. She spoke to Michael about this but Michael said it wasn't all the time, and anyway it meant that they had more time together sitting on the sofa and being close. The angrier Delia got about it, the more Michael dug in his heels. He said it was none of her business what he did in his own home. The argument continued.

When Fay and Will split up, their children were 22 months and three years old. Will had not mastered cooking and the kids ended up eating fast food. Fay had always maintained a healthy household and was really concerned that the children were consuming too much fat and sugar, and she told Will so. Will said that it wouldn't hurt them and he had no intention of wasting his time cooking when he could be having fun with his kids. It was his business what he did when he had the kids.

When George and Tina split up their children were 14 and 16. George was their main carer as Tina travelled a great deal for work, so the children lived with George and visited their mother. When George grounded one of their teenagers and it overlapped into time spent at their mother's, he expected Tina to keep to the punishment. Tina was adamant that she would not. She did not see the kids that often, and when she did they would go out and do things together. She had no intention of keeping to George's rules. He could enforce them on his time, not hers.

Sound familiar? You can put in your own story around behaviour, discipline, food, language, whatever you choose. The fact is that when you parent apart you have absolutely no control over how the other parents. Unless you have evidence of mental or physical cruelty, or specific times when your children were put into dangerous situations, my advice is 'Get over it.' Your children will survive. So what if they eat fast food for a couple of days, go to bed late or get away with something you would not allow? They will live to tell the tale.

While you are experiencing frustration over what you have no control over, your children are easily picking up that what works for one parent doesn't necessarily work for the other. When children go to school they experience being in classes with different teachers. These teachers have different tolerance levels and expect different types of behaviour. Kids learn to adapt. This is great, because that's exactly what they will have to learn to do in the real world when they're grown up.

Your children will make their own decisions about what works and what doesn't, what's right and what's wrong all by themselves, and you cannot escape their judgements about you and the way you parent them. My advice is to keep your own standards and walk your own talk. Model the behaviour you would like your children to emulate. As Ghandi said 'be the change you want to see in the world.' So, unless you want to drive yourself and your children mad, give it up, let it go and get on with parenting your own way.

> *'We are divorced, we are friends and*
> *we are good parents.'* – **Sarah Ferguson**

Parenting Plans that Work
Having said all this, very many parents create wonderful parenting plans and find themselves easily singing from the same hymn sheet. They agree about most things to do with the children and are able to decide together the best route forward. Sarah Ferguson is a great example of staying more than amicable with Prince Andrew. Never once have we heard her complain in any way. OK, she has the financial resources that

most of us can only dream about, but as we know from the media this doesn't deter some people from taking every opportunity to make life so difficult for their ex-partner that, inevitably, their children suffer.

In my own situation, being the best parent I could be for my kids and making sure they had their dad in their lives was vitally important. Mostly our arrangements worked well. My husband left all the school stuff and medical appointments to me and I kept him informed. In turn he always kept to his agreements about seeing the children and picking them up when he said he would. We were not in a sound financial situation and there could have been arguments over money, but I chose not to dwell on what I didn't have and be grateful for what I did have. As the saying goes, if life gives you lemons, make lemonade. There are two ways of doing this. Easy or hard. It's your choice.

Make some time to sit down with your ex to create a working plan together. You may decide to review it after a month or several weeks, and in that case, put a date in both your diaries to meet up or speak on the phone to do this.

Ideally, your parenting plan should cover the following areas:

Keeping Each Other Informed

Each parent should keep the other informed about doctor's appointments, illness, school-related activities, parent evenings and news from teachers about how your child is doing at school. If your child has challenges, put aside your own disputes and *talk* (yes, I did say talk) about how best to serve your child. Both of you will have different ideas and both ways will have their merits. Be adult enough to combine the two and create a win-win for your child.

Contact Arrangements

If you can make the contact arrangements together, that's ⟨...⟩ ⟨...⟩s to go through the courts, then at least everyone knows where ⟨...⟩y stand. Whichever way, you'll have to come to a resolution in the end, so unless you want to throw your own money away, take your emotions out of the situation and do it yourselves. The only reason for not sticking to your agreement is if some dire emergency stops you.

I urge you to keep your word around your contact arrangements. First, because of the impact it has on your child if you don't, and second, so that you can build some trust between you and your ex. You need to be able to rely on each other. This may be the first time in years that you can trust each other to do anything. But this is about the children and cannot be compared to your own relationship.

Holidays

Christmas, holidays and religious holy days must be shared. It's simple. You have them one year, your ex the following. When my children were young they would have Christmas Eve with me and their dad would come over on Christmas morning to open presents and either leave if he was seeing them the next day or take them with him after present opening. You may not be on good enough terms to do this, but again, put your personal grudges aside and do what's best and most fair for your children.

Family and Friends

If you had a close relationship with your ex-partner's family, even if you stop seeing them your children will need to. Grandparents are especially important because they offer the patience and love that being able to give a child back at the end of the day brings. They also give children a sense of history and identity as well as a healthy respect for the older generation. Then there are aunties and uncles and cousins, all of whom form a supportive network for your children. Once again, unless you have reason to believe that there are physical or emotional safety issues around any of these people, allow your children to be part of their lives. They may have religious beliefs or ways of behaving that you disagree with. Trust that your own continuous modelling of your own beliefs and values at home will be taken on board by your children and the diversity they experience away from you is an energy that they will enjoy and be able to make their own decisions about when they are older.

Blame

It may happen that your kids have an accident while they are with you. You tell your ex because you have agreed to inform each other of things like this. He says you are irresponsible and always in a hurry and if you'd just slowed down Daisy would not have fallen out of the shopping trolley (ouch!). You say, well, if I didn't have to rush from work to pick up the kids from the child minder, do the shopping, get them home in time for tea and then go to my second job in the evening it wouldn't have happened (you good-for-nothing 'bleep'!).

Please don't play *the blame game*. It does you no good. Why add hurt to hurt, pain to pain and try to win points at your child's expense? Just tell each other what you have done to clear up whatever mess has been made, and let each other off the hook.

Transitions

A specific time that both of you will find most upsetting is the transition period when you have picked your child up from your ex or you receive your child back home after they have visited your ex.

Children of all ages are uncomfortable with being 'suitcase kids'. Packing up their belongings to leave, unpacking at both ends, forgetting their favourite book, toy, iPod or hair straighteners is not much fun. If you can afford to keep some doubles of uniform or at least pyjamas, that helps, but it's not always possible. Understand that this is an unsettling and disturbing time for them. They have once again left one parent for another. There may even be feelings of betrayal towards one parent, if they were longing to come home to you and they believe they are supposed to love both parents equally. There are a few ways to handle this, but first and foremost *expect it to happen*.

Younger Children

When you pick them up or they are dropped back home, there may be tears. Don't adopt a cheerful 'It's all OK' attitude. It isn't OK. Hold them or give them a hug and acknowledge that 'It's really hard to leave Daddy and come back home. It feels really sad to say goodbye, doesn't it?' Your child will begin to feel listened to and understood, and this means that these episodes will gradually lose their intensity in the future.

Another option is to do something with them straight away, like take them out to the park, pop into the supermarket for a couple of items just to change the scenery, put them in the bath to splash around or just let them have their tantrum, be quiet or be a little clingy for a while. It's just behaviour – don't judge it or make it mean that you are a terrible person for doing this to them. Unless, of course, you want to. Then do feel free to beat yourself up for as long as you wish!

Older Children

During the teenage years a typical transition period might involve coming in, going straight to their rooms, slamming doors or switching on the TV and not speaking for a while. I was respectful enough to let it happen with my children, and in their own good time they would come and talk to me. Older children need space. When mine would come into the kitchen after their cooling-off period we would generally have a hug that kind of said it all, and they were back in the fold once again.

Personally, I have always experienced a transition period with my children, and even now that my daughter is 22 it still persists. She may drive her own car to her dad's and back again, or go to meet him for a meal, but she often comes back with some sort of upset. My son is less vocal but adopts a resigned attitude. They have unfulfilled expectations that have no answers. I don't know how long this will go on, but I do know that it's their stuff to work on. It's not about me, it's about the relationship they have with their dad and there is nothing I can do about that, apart from empathize and be there to listen if they need that from me.

What We All Want for Our Children

We all want to raise happy, healthy children who have high levels of self-esteem and confidence, who are truthful, loving, fully self-expressed and well adjusted. In order to do this, we need to respect each other's feelings and experiences and not devalue them in any way. We need to commit ourselves to resolve any conflicts that arise between us in a way that allows us both to win and neither to lose at the other's expense. In order to relate to our children with empathy, love and respect, we need to teach them by example what that looks like.

Times When You Simply Cannot Listen to Your Children

There will be times when you simply don't have the emotional or physical capacity to listen to your kids. Perhaps you are too tired after a long day at work, perhaps you are too involved in the problem they are going through or are having a problem of your own. You may be late for work or busy preparing dinner and have no time in that moment, or maybe you're just not feeling accepting of your child. There are ways to handle this.

You could say, 'I'm sorry, I'm having trouble listening, I'm so tired that I can't concentrate and I know this is important to you. Let's talk about it tomorrow/after dinner.'

Or how about, 'I'm too worried/upset/scared/cross to listen. Give me some time to calm down and then I will try to understand.'

Other options are, 'I have to leave for work, but I do want to talk to you about this. Can we talk about it (at whatever time)?' or 'I'm finding it hard to want to listen to this, but I would like to work it out. How could we do this? (This question is for an older child or an adult with whom you want to share the responsibility for the issue together.)

The fact is that you can only listen if the following attitudes are in place:

- You really do want to understand the other person.
- You feel accepting of them right now.
- You feel accepting of yourself right now.
- You genuinely care about the other's feelings.
- You can allow the other person to express sad, angry or scared feelings without jumping in with a judgement or a solution.

When these attitudes are in place you are more able to listen.

In Chapter 4, I explained the listening skills that you can use with your ex-partner. Please also use these with your children and everybody else in your life to help you communicate effectively and avoid upset and misunderstandings.

The Opportunity (or the Gift in the Garbage!)

Divorce offers all of us an opportunity to be even better parents than we could ever have been as a couple. The reason for this is that we get to spend more time with our children alone. They see who we are and we see who they are. They judge us on our merits and we cannot hide behind the other parent. We are fully exposed and absolutely vulnerable. I have seen fathers become closer with their children than they ever were during marriage. I have experienced holidays with my children on their own, having adventures that would never have been possible with my husband.

After 14 years I am so proud of who my wonderful children have become. Their compassion, their love, their work ethic and their kindness are all as a result of the life they have led because they were children of divorce. Would they have been better off if their parents had stayed together? Who knows?

What I do know is that, for you and your ex and your children, this is not the end of the world but the beginning of a different one that has the potential for creating outstanding children who will grow into understanding adults – adults who, because of their experiences, can make a huge contribution to their own lives and the lives of all the people they meet.

Personal Prescription for Effective Parenting in Divorce: Five-day Treatment

Directions for Use

You are required to spend the next five days becoming more aware of your children's behaviours and noticing your attitude and response to them.

This may be quite painful and at other times quite empowering. As you observe yourself in relationship with your children, you will realize just how much power you have to influence their feelings and their experience of your divorce, just through the way you react to what happens on a daily basis. Your reactions and how you interact with your ex will be observed by your children, and they will make up what divorce is all about by watching how you handle it.

Dosage

For the next five days, keep a daily note in your Divorce Diary of:

- What challenges there have been with your children that day.
- How did you react? What was your attitude?
- What specific actions did you take to address the situation?

Doing this on a daily basis will allow you to build your confidence as an effective parent during this difficult time for all of you. As you continue to monitor your own emotional temperature, find creative ways to handle the issues that affect your children. You'll grow as a parent and become a great example for your kids.

The Self-affirmation Medicine

Choose three affirmations each day and repeat each of them three times each per day for five consecutive days.

- I am a fabulous and courageous parent.
- I respect my children and am able to step into their world.
- I know my own boundaries and I am fully self-expressed. When I am unable to listen or communicate effectively I will tell my children the reason. I will then take responsibility for making a mutually convenient time to do so.
- I am learning when to speak and when to listen.
- I am letting go of guilt and replacing it with love.
- Today I will be the best parent I can be.

Part 3
Scrubbing Up for Life Apart

Chapter 6
Financial Fitness

Awareness Of your financial situation
Attitude Choosing to face facts
Action Taking responsible actions that lead to financial wellbeing

We've learned how to manage your ex; we've sorted out your kids. Now it's time for *you*. Your new life is beckoning and it's time to get practical and take actions that will move you towards a secure and fulfilling future that gives you the time to live your life the way you want it to be.

Money Matters

One of the most important areas is, of course, finance. For many people, their deepest desire after divorce is to make themselves as financially independent as possible. It's not that money necessarily brings happiness. There are some incredibly rich divorcees who would rather be in a great relationship than in Harrods shopping. But money pays the bills, gives us choices and allows us to honour our own standards. However scary it may all seem, you simply have to learn how to handle it.

I can remember the fear and panic that overwhelmed me when I thought about the reality of having to be responsible for my finances. Having never had to pay a bill for 15 years, as my husband always dealt with the finances, I was dizzy even thinking about how I would manage. I remember standing in the queue at the supermarket wondering if I had budgeted correctly as the total kept escalating after each item. Often I had to leave things behind, and I've even on occasion cleaned my loo with washing-up liquid because I couldn't afford toothpaste *and* toilet cleaner. So I understand how difficult this can be for so many people. It can be a steep learning curve.

In order to enjoy a healthy attitude to money, you have to understand your current feelings about it and how to make it work for you. Part of your return to full vibrant health includes you becoming financially fit so that you can take back control of your life. I think one of the greatest freedoms of my entire life is being in control of my own finances. It's also one of my biggest personal responsibilities, but the fact is that I have grown in a way that I never would have done during marriage. I take 100 per cent personal responsibility for my own financial well-being, and I love it.

Limbering Up

Financial fitness is not necessarily about taking three jobs and working every hour God sends. It is possible that you will have to work in a way that was not necessary before your divorce, but the trick is to find a way of working smarter, not necessarily harder. You need to use all the fabulous resources you already have available and hone them so that they give you the best possible return on your investment of time on a daily basis.

> Jennifer had been married to Harry for 18 years. During that time Harry's finances had been pretty unstable. Harry had various jobs, none of them lasted for long and money was unpredictable, but he was an eternal optimist and always thought that something would turn up just when they needed it. Luckily Jennifer owned their very large house, inherited from her parents, so she always felt their home

was secure. However, five years ago Jennifer discovered that Harry had been gambling all their married life. He had been very clever at hiding it, but when Jennifer was refused a credit card she became suspicious, and her investigations uncovered that he had been forging her signature to obtain credit in various forms and had personal debts of over £112,000. With no credit available and debts mounting, Jennifer decided to see a lawyer.

As it turned out, even though Harry had forged her signature, as his wife she was liable for his debts. It took her laywer a while to sort out the paper trail, which uncovered a series of other deceptions. After a two-year battle, Jennifer now lives in a small terraced house with her two boys and her divorce from Harry is complete.

Whilst she has much less than she started with, her lawyer helped her achieve the peace of mind that comes with being in control of her own life.

In cases where your ex-partner has deceived you or dumped their debts on you, it is vital that you seek professional help and be clear about your rights at every stage. I have listed some exceptionally competent lawyers with whom I personally work in the resources section at the end of the book.

For those couples who want to maintain the most amicable of relationships after divorce, or whose split is a joint decision, or where assets are minimal and perhaps there are children involved, the next step could well be mediation. I have listed mediators that I use in the resources section; your local citizens advice bureau will have names of others in your area.

My Financial Guru

In the early years of being single again, I struggled with understanding my finances and turned to an amazing 'wealth coach' and friend, Grainne O'Malley. Grainne understands the psychology of money and how to make your money work for you. She has been through her own emotional roller coaster with money and now teaches men and women fresh out of divorce how to do the same. Her book *More than Money* can be read in a couple of hours and is an investment for life. Using everything she has learned over the past 25 years she now runs seminars for people who are ready and willing to face up to and take control of their finances. As she says, 'If you don't understand your finances, they just haven't been explained to you properly yet.' The best advice I can give you is to read her book.

Money Is an Emotional Business

When I first got divorced I was incredibly scared of the responsibility of handling all the bills and managing my money effectively. Although I had lived on my own before marrying, I'd always had to juggle, and the thought of doing this again was frightening.

In the early days of our living apart, knowing that I struggled in this area, my ex devised a system of envelopes for me. I was supposed to allocate my money for bills and other outgoings into separate envelopes so I would know exactly what was supposed to go where. At the end of each month, however, I'd be in a real mess and would sit on the floor with my envelopes and cry. Why was I crying? Not just because I was a wimp. It's because *money is an emotional issue*. It's not about envelopes, pieces of paper and coins, it's about what money means to us. For me it was about being looked after and being able to depend and rely on someone to handle this stuff.

After a couple of very difficult years, I attended a seminar about our attitude to money and what it means to us. The question we were asked was, 'If money came to tea, how would you greet it?' I remember

thinking that I'd be quite surprised that 'he' had co
for me money is male!) and then I'd say 'How long
And money would say, 'Not long' and scoot out the ba.   _fore
drinking his tea! Learning this about myself was a catalyst ..oment for
me. It was obvious to me that my relationship with money was one of
scarcity rather than abundance. I knew that I had to work on my own
beliefs about money and discover where these beliefs came from so that
I could create a far more effective attitude towards it.

Before we go any further I'd like you to ask yourself the same question.
Your answer will give you an insight into your own beliefs and attitude
towards money, and you may be surprised at what you learn.

So, if money came to tea, how would you greet it?

- What would you say?
- What would money say?
- How would you feel?
- Then what would happen?

So what *did* happen when money arrived? Did you think 'Of course you
are here,' 'Hello, good friend' or 'Thank you for coming'? 'Darjeeling
or Earl Grey?' Did you welcome money with open arms or did money
arrive through the front door only to slip out the back? Did it settle
in and stay a while? Did you lock it up and keep it prisoner? Did you
wonder why it had even knocked on your door?

Your emotional reaction to money will make dealing with it easy,
challenging or difficult. Your job is to understand where your attitude
comes from so that you are in a position to make new choices that will
empower you and motivate you instead of holding you back.

Here are some of the questions that Grainne asked me before we even began to put pen to paper and draw up budgets or accounts. Answering these questions will show you how you've created your beliefs about money.

Your History of Money

1. What did you learn from your father about money?
2. What did you learn from your mother about money?
3. What did you learn about money at school?
4. Are the people who shaped you financially, financially secure themselves?
5. What patterns do you have around money that get you into trouble?
6. What does money mean to you?
7. What do you believe about yourself and money?

Grainne then gave me some really good advice. She said, 'Love where you are at until you get where you are going.' This allowed me to stop beating myself up about my old beliefs about money and begin to use my past relationship with money as a place to learn from. I began making distinctions. I began to see that if I carried on in the same vein, nothing much would change, but if I learned new skills and strategies around money I could be in control of my own life so that I never need be frightened about the future again. Knowledge is power – for me it gave me the power to decide what I wanted, what I needed and what I would be willing to do to satisfy both areas.

Change Your Habits – Change Your Life

So let's look at the next set of questions that Grainne gave me. Take your time to answer them for yourself. Dig deep and write your answers down.

- What will it mean to you if you change your financial habits now and take charge of your financial life?
- What will it really mean for your future to be comfortable and confident in handling your money?
- Who do you want to become financially?
- What will you be able to give yourself and those you care for?
- What experiences will you be able to have and what experiences will you be able to share with others?
- Close your eyes for a moment and see yourself in 12 months having taken control of your money. How does that feel?
- See yourself in 5 years and 10 and 20 years. How would your life be different if you took control of yourself financially, starting right now?
- Write your answers down in less than 10 minutes. Do it *now* before you read any more of this chapter.
- Now take a look at your answers. As you read them, imagine yourself in 5, 10 and 20 years NOT having taken control of your finances.
- What will your life be like if you just keep on doing what you have been doing up to now?
- What will that cost you?
- What will it do to your health, your relationships, and your day-to-day life?
- What things or experiences will you never have?
- How does that future feel to you?

Don't Reinvent the Wheel

What I learned from Grainne is not to make life hard for myself. She said 'Everyone knows someone who is great with money.'

Think about someone you know who handles money in exactly they way you'd like to. What results do they get financially that you would like to achieve? What do they do differently that gives them results? Yes, they probably have different beliefs about money than you do, but now you understand where your beliefs come from you have the power to decide to do things differently. Getting divorced is an opportunity to make different choices. Looking at someone who is financially fit and following some of their basic strategies to achieve the same goals is a good start.

Spending Money

Just as we were getting closer to looking at the numbers that told the story of my financial situation, Grainne asked me to do something else. She said that every time I went to spend money I should **STOP!**

I was to ask myself if I was spending it because I thought it was a good idea or if it was just something I had always done, or something I had seen my parents doing which I had unconsciously picked up. In this way I began to notice my own habits. I was already quite frugal and a fairly good saver, but could easily be spontaneous and indulgent. As money was tight, I decided to create a rule for myself around my own personal spending habits. I would not buy anything for myself that I didn't absolutely love. If I was in any doubt, I'd walk away to give myself time to really decide if I could live without whatever it was. Just taking myself out of the shop was enough to change my mental and physical state and make a much wiser decision.

In the days and weeks to come, apply this strategy to your own spending habits. Get back in control instead of allowing the lure of 'more things' to give you a momentary 'feel-good' feeling.

Let's Get Practical

Grainne explained to me that income has two main purposes:

1. It pays for your current lifestyle
2. It contributes to your future.

Back then, I was much more concerned with my current lifestyle and getting through the week, but Grainne explained that unless I understood how to spend less than I earn, I would never be able to prepare for my future. On top of this, she suggested that I regularly put 10 per cent of my income aside into a high-interest account. She suggested that I pay this to myself as my first and most important expense, and then take care of my other expenses. It's one of the easiest routes to financial independence.

Expenses

Take a look at the following list. These are the kinds of expenses you will have. Some are monthly and some are yearly. I'd like you to get a notebook and list these expenses, calculating from memory what you spend on each item every month. If it's holidays, calculate what you might spend and divide by 12 to get the monthly amount. At this point we don't need to be exact.

Bank charges	Gifts/presents	Petrol
Books/mags	Groceries	Rates
Car insurance	Hobbies	Rent/mortgage
Car maintenance	Holidays	Restaurant
Car tax	Household equipment	School fees
Car loan	House insurance	Stationery/postage
Charitable contributions	House maintenance/décor	Sport
Christmas	Investments (list each one)	Sundry expenses
Cleaning	Kids' care	Taxes
Clothing	Kids' clothing	Telephone
Courses	Kids' toys	Travel
Credit card interest	Legal/professional fees	Toiletries
Dentist	Medical expenses/insurance	TV licence
Electricity	Music	Water rates
Fuel (home)	Personal care	Loans
Gas	Pet care	

When you multiply the total amount you spend each month by 12, you get your yearly expenses. If your yearly expenses are *less* than your income then you have a 'monthly net profit'. If your yearly expenses are *more* than your income, then you have a 'monthly net loss'.

If you find you have a monthly net loss, don't panic. Knowing the truth about your income and outgoings, however scary, means you now have the opportunity to come up with solutions instead of losing sleep worrying about something you are unsure of.

The next task Grainne showed me is how to divide my expenses into the following four categories:

1. **Must Haves (MH)**

    MHs are those expense items without which your life would not function, such as food and accommodation and utilities

2. **Nice to Haves (NTH)**

    NTHs are those items that you could do without if you had to, such as pot pourri or scented candles

3. **Investments (I)**

Is are those items that you get some kind of return on, such as pensions

4. **Debt Repayments (DR)**

DRs are monies to repay debt such as loan payments, credit card payments or car payments.

The Key to MHs

We all have to pay our rent or mortgage and utility bills and feed ourselves. And some people must use their car for work or to get to work, so your car, car tax, congestion charge (in London) and insurance are vital.

Less obvious yet equally vital are some of those items that would definitely not make a standard accounting MH. These are items that don't just feed our bodies; they feed our minds and our spirit.

Personally if I don't go to at least one personal development seminar a year, have my nails done regularly and retain my gym membership, I would be happy to throw in the towel. There are some things that make life worth living, release stress, re-energize us and give us the will to carry on another day. Whatever it is for you, it falls into the category of a Must Have, so own up to it.

The point is that you know what is vital to you. Most of us will find that 90 per cent of our lists are similar. We have similar basic needs. The other 10 per cent will be down to the individual and will reflect who you are and what is important to you. These are what you must have in order to feel that you are living and not just existing. So what is it for you?

- Mark all your MHs in one colour with a highlighter.
- Mark all your Is in a second colour
- Next mark your DRs
- The remainder are your NTHs.

Now take your NTH list and go through them one by one.

- Tick the ones that you are paying for that are no longer pleasurable enough to be worth spending your hard-earned cash (or maintenance money) on.
- Tick the ones that you feel guilty paying for (such as a gym membership you never use). Ask yourself for each one, 'Is this item worth more than my future financial security?'
- When you have examined how you feel about each NTH, make a list of the items you want to drop.
- Add up the amount of money you will save by doing this.

Congratulations, you have just improved your net income by this amount EVERY month. This means you are already on your way to creating your 10 per cent that will go towards the freedom of future financial independence.

Time Is Money

Time is something I am a bit of an expert about, having delivered training in time management to large corporations for many years. In my book *Time to Live* I point out that the most successful people in the world 'spend' their time wisely. Isn't it interesting that we talk about how we 'spend' our time? Literally every moment of our time, once 'spent', is gone and can never be retrieved. An example of this for me is when I am stuck in traffic. I hate wasting time doing that because in my head I often calculate how much my time is worth and what it has cost me to waste it. But have you ever thought about your purchases in terms of the time it takes you to earn the money?

Recently I went shopping to cheer myself up after an upset. I saw a great pair of shoes – obviously a Must Have. I bought them and paid for them. Grainne points out that this relates specifically to time:

- **How did I afford the shoes?** *I went to work.*
- **And why did I go to work?** *To earn the money that bought the shoes.*

So the shoes are, in effect, worth a specific number of minutes or hours of my time.

Money Is Time

I asked myself, 'Was it worth the spend?' Were the shoes worth a half day of my life spent at work? (They were expensive shoes!)

The point is that every working hour has a value which is part of your financial picture. Knowing how much your time is worth will help you decide where and when to spend your money.

Can you really *afford* your 'must haves'? Are your 'must haves' a replacement for something else you are not getting? If they are, what is it that's really missing from your life and what would you need in order to fill the gap? Something to think about!

Debt Is Not the Problem – Repaying Debt Is

One of the scariest places to be after divorce is in debt. Whether they are debts you created or debts your ex created that you 'inherited', your first target has to be the total elimination of that debt.

I am not an expert on debt and the first thing I would stress is that if you have debts that are frightening you, you need to speak to someone who specializes in this area. I have listed a company I recommend at the back of the book who are specialists; you may have others in your area. However, what I will also show you is Grainne's basic strategy for eliminating debt. It's a step-by-step method I use to this day.

- List each debt you have, showing the total you owe, the amount you pay per month and the number of payments left.
- Pick one of them that you would really like to pay off. Call it Debt No. 1. (Do not pick your mortgage.) What date is the last payment of the debt you have chosen?
- Can you find £75-£100 per month from your current income that you can pay as extra towards that debt every month? You may think it's impossible, but if you don't find it, it will take much longer to repay your debt.
- Look at what happens if you add the extra money to your monthly payment for Debt No. 1
- How many payments will you have to make to eliminate that debt now? Notice the difference. (If you can work it out, also notice the amount of interest you have saved by repaying the debt off more quickly.)
- Now here's the bit I really love.

- When you have paid off Debt No. 1, take the monthly amount you were paying towards it *plus* the £75–£100 and put that amount towards Debt No. 2 until it is paid off. Do the same with any remaining debts and you will eliminate the next debt really quickly, and so on until you are debt free.

Once you have paid off your debts, you can begin to think about something that will give you the peace of mind that comes from true financial fitness: the Emergency Fund.

What Is an Emergency Fund?

An Emergency Fund is just that: a fund that you keep for emergencies. Most of us jog along each month covering our expenses and staying ahead until something happens. It could be anything. Perhaps you need sick leave or you lose your job or you choose to change your job. Any situation that occurs which means you have a short period of reduced income or inconsistent income can put you in a pressurized situation.

The key to financial peace of mind and being able to sleep at night without financial worries is to have a little put aside. Just how much should that be? Well, everyone is different. For me it's a fund of three months' money.

The added bonus of having Emergency Fund Money is that just knowing this money is there, should you need it, allows you to sleep well each night and have a Plan B in place should you need it.

If you follow the guidelines above, you will become financially fit and ready for your new life.

Personal Prescription for Financial Fitness: Five-day Observation Treatment

Directions for Use

1. You are required to observe your attitude to money. Look at your beliefs and where they come from. Ask yourself if these beliefs and attitudes serve you and if not, what you are willing to do to change them. Observe yourself shopping in the supermarket, in the mall, on the internet. Notice your thought processes as you decide to purchase or not purchase specific items.

2. You are required to become consistent when handling money.

Dosage

Work towards the following:

- Spending less than you earn and having a monthly net profit
- Putting 10 per cent of your income aside each month to contribute towards your future
- Having a plan to repay debt
- Putting cash aside in an emergency fund.

Self-affirmation Medicine

The following affirmations must be repeated at least 10 times each, three times per day for five consecutive days.

- Money is a friend who is always by my side.
- Money flows freely and abundantly into my life.
- I create my own security.
- I always have more money coming in than going out.
- I know my value and honour my worth.
- I spend my money wisely.

Chapter 7
Taking Charge of Your Career

Awareness	Of your most valuable skills
Attitude	Belief in what you have to offer
Action	How to align what you do with what others need

Whether you already have a job or a career path, or don't work and haven't done for many years, work may now be more important financially than it was when you were married. Divorce changes everything, so why not use the opportunity to make some really big improvements to your career?

Going back to Work

When I was first divorced and returning to work, I knew that I didn't want to go back to being a secretary because I hadn't really been all that good at it. I knew I had to work, but I wanted to do something fulfilling that expressed who I was. I had nearly completed my counselling training and had been to the USA to study parent effectiveness training, and was already running classes, but it would not have earned me enough money to live on without working a paid job.

I was aware enough to know that I was now on my own journey towards personal fulfilment, and anything I worked at from that point on had to satisfy me in my mind *and* my pocket. I wanted to look forward to going to work knowing that what I did made a real difference to other people's lives. In order to do that I had to make some changes to my whole belief system and add to my knowledge base. Perhaps you are interested in doing the same? I want you to find the work you love because, after all, if you are responsible for bringing home the bacon you may as well love what you do.

The Purpose of Your Work

It's absolutely vital to know your purpose in life if you are to live a fulfilled, satisfied and contented life. Not only that, in order to be in a healthy relationship in the future, you must first be an individual with a separate identity of your own. If you are not you will always be looking to the other person to fill a gap inside you, and they will always fail. One of the ways to create your own identity and fulfil your purpose is through the work you do.

Your life purpose is not something saint-like. You are not aiming to be Mother Teresa or Ghandi. Your life purpose is about taking the qualities, characteristics and natural talents you possess and channelling them in a way that meets the needs of other people and provides you with an income. In offering your talents in exchange for hard currency, you gain a feeling of being valued for who you are and what you do, and you experience the fulfilment of making a difference and contributing to others.

> *'When what you do and who you are meet the needs of the world, therein lies your vocation.'* **- Aristotle**

It may be that your purpose in life is to be a caring community member, teach martial arts or be a landscape gardener. It may have a more spiritual base. I have no idea what it is for you, but I do know that if you drift through life without having some idea of what you are here for, there will be an emptiness inside that will never be filled. Strong stuff? Well, don't take my word for it. Look at what Aristotle had to say in three hundred years BC. This is not some new-age idea. Personal fulfilment is the ultimate stage of wellness and provides exceptional emotional and physical health.

When you are living out your life purpose, you don't have to try to be something you are not. You are free to be who you are and express yourself in a way that serves you and others. We may not yet know what it is or how to express it, or maybe we've simply forgotten over the years what it was.

It usually takes something like divorce or bereavement or some other catalyst event for people to realize that life is not just about doing or being what other people want. Who we were in the past simply doesn't fit with who we are now and we need to make changes in order to continue to grow.

So this is not just about taking control of your career. This is about finding out what you are passionate about. It's about creating results that bring you the joy and fulfilment you are seeking. It's about getting back to you and your inner spirit, to the place that has all the answers if you will only take the time to listen.

Dying with Your Music Inside

Mary was 89 when I met her. She was in a care home in Bournemouth and I was 14 and part of a youth group who visited the elderly to entertain them or simply spend time with them. I sat down on one of those brown high-backed institution chairs next to this petite little lady and the first thing she said to me was, 'You know, I could have been a ballerina.' 'Could you?' I asked. Mary nodded and said that she had been a very talented dancer, but then her mother had died and, as the eldest, she was needed to look after her father and her three brothers and two sisters. She said, 'Things were different in those days.' What struck me, though, was that Mary had never forgotten her dream. Mary might not have reached the heights of Margot Fonteyn but she might have gone on to teach ballet or be part of that world. She couldn't do it back then, but you can. And when you are in your rocking chair, aged 89, do you imagine you will have forgotten your dreams? I wouldn't bet on it.

Doing the Work You Love

So how do you rediscover your purpose in life? It's already there and always has been. It's just been lying dormant.

How do you access your passion and use it to achieve personal fulfilment, contribute to others and bring you prosperity?

Your Rules for Life

Your values are your specific rules for life. They are the set of operating instructions your parents should have received at your birth. These instructions would have told them exactly how to handle you, what makes you tick, how to get the best out of you, what buttons not to press and how best to love you and show you how much you are appreciated and valued. As you grew up, you would have been able to give these instructions to your friends, your partners and your own children, and in turn you would have received theirs and everyone would be very clear about what each of us needs and wants. As if!

Even though that didn't happen, however, it doesn't mean it cannot happen now. You have full permission to rewrite the rules for every area of your life. Now is the time to gain clarity about yourself so that you can explain yourself to the other people in your life and build great relationships.

Right now we are going to concentrate on a specific value that we will call 'Ultimate Ideal Career'. Your 'Ultimate Ideal Career' value will give you an amazing amount of information that you can use towards rediscovering your life purpose. So let's begin.

Using the template below, I'd like you to fill in your own definitions of your ideal career. I have given some examples, but take some time to really think about your answers as you fill in each of the definitions.

Values = 'Must Haves'	Definitions
	What would [an Ultimate Ideal Career] provide me with? What would have to happen in order for me to experience [an Ultimate Ideal Career]? What am I willing to do to achieve [an Ultimate Ideal Career] and when will I begin? What would happen if I didn't have [an Ultimate Ideal Career]?
My Ultimate Ideal Career	What would my Ultimate Ideal Career provide me with?: using my creativity/success/feeling that I was doing what I do best/be able to write/be able to design/be able to make music/be able to teach/appreciation/value/respect/ acknowledgement from my peers/contribution to others/ changing the way people feel about themselves ... etc.

What would have to happen in order for me to experience an Ultimate Ideal Career?: I'd have to believe I could do it/I'd have to have some money behind me/I'd have to retrain/I'd have to study in the evenings/I'd have to speak to my friend who owns a company that does what I want to do and see if I can get some experience before I decide/I'd have to get a bank loan/I'd have to believe I was doing what I love ... etc.

What does my Ultimate Ideal Career provide others with?: the opportunity to think about what is true for them/ pleasure in their homes by enjoying my designs/ inspiration from my music ... etc.

What am I willing to do to achieve an Ultimate Ideal Career and when will I do it?: |

	I'd have to decide what my first steps were and take them/I'd have to speak to (whomever) to help me get started/I'd have to ask my boss for time off to study/I'd have to act now/next week/next month (whenever, but put a date on it) … etc. What would happen if I didn't experience an Ultimate Ideal Career?: I'd just plod along where I am now/become resentful/be jealous of others who made it/be upset with my restrictions/never feel fulfilled/be dead inside/take it out on my partner/I'd have to find a way of doing something that moved me towards it.

You now have more insight into what doing work you love would mean to you. When you ask yourself 'What would my Ultimate Ideal Career provide for me?' your answers reflect your values. For example, if you say 'creativity' or 'communication', then if you can honour these values on a daily basis, you will make your life wonderful. When these values are *not* met in your working life (and probably in other areas of your life, too) it comes as no surprise that you will experience upset or pain.

> Here is something to think about:
> It's never the person, the situation or the circumstance that will ever upset or frustrate me, it's always a value of mine that has been dishonoured or violated.

What this means is that, while we may think that others have upset us, or that situations, events or environments have conspired to irritate us, what's actually happening is that values that we hold dear – such as respect, appreciation, being valued for who we are, free self-expression, security or consideration – have been trodden on. We don't just feel the pain and indignation of our own squashed feelings, it's like someone has devalued our identity.

When we are able to identify which of our values has been violated, even our communication changes. We are able to let the other person know why we are reacting as we are. We can explain how we feel, using words that describe our values, which means that we will be heard more easily and understood.

The next question, 'What would have to happen in order for me to have my Ultimate Ideal Career?', begins to look at what you believe is possible. Remember the voices of sabotage and alert? Be careful here. Yes, the 'alert' may be realizing that there are specific actions to take if you are to achieve your goal, such as gaining more skills or experience. However, there may also be some self-sabotage going on to stop you from stepping out of your comfort zone. You need to be able to make a distinction between the two.

The next definition is 'What does my Ultimate Ideal Career provide others with?' This is about contributing. This is where many people would say ultimate fulfilment lies. How wonderful to be doing something you love *and* making a difference to people's lives.

When coaching came to the UK about 14 years ago, it was challenging to become recognized as a life coach. People had never heard of it, nor did they think they needed it. I struggled hard to create my practice in the early years, and only my unshakeable belief in the fantastic results my clients were achieving kept me from throwing in the towel.

Be very clear about what your career or business provides for other people. People buy benefits, not products or services. Most people do not need drills, they need holes. They don't want mortgages, they want homes. Sell holes and sell homes. Sell benefits. If you can do that, you will achieve your ultimate fulfilment when people tell you the difference you have made to their lives.

The question, 'What am I willing to do to achieve my Ultimate Ideal Career and when will I do it?' begins to hold you accountable for your choice. This is your 'put your money where your mouth is' moment. Are you actually willing to retrain? Are you really willing to ask for help? Are you willing to declare your intention to whoever needs to know and ask for help where it's needed? The following process can help to reveal the answers.

Skills List

Your first task is to compile a list of all your current skills. Write down everything you are capable of doing, from changing light bulbs to organizing events, from redecorating or managing a hedge fund to running a team of 50 people, and every skill in between. Don't forget what a great parent you are, fabulous friend and family member.

Look at your list and ask yourself what each of your skills provides you with. Does it give you a sense of status? Do you receive acknowledgement? Does it evoke feelings of excitement and inspiration? Do these skills light up your life and motivate you to jump out of bed in the morning? If you don't experience a positive feeling from some of your current skills, they are probably not skills you personally value, however much other people may need them or however much money they create for you.

Make a list of the skills that honour your values. Start thinking outside the box. How could you combine skills to create your ideal career? A career that would serve not only you but others, too?

When Stephanie came to me she had just split up with Louis after seven years of marriage. She had twin boys of five who were just about to start school and she was ready to use her free hours to produce more income for the family. Louis was great with his maintenance payments but it still was not enough to manage on now that they had separate households. Stephanie had trained to become a life coach but was ready to give it up because she felt so isolated working on her own. When we looked at her skill base, we realized that she loved the work she was doing but working from home was depressing her and her work was suffering. Stephanie was an outdoors person. She lived in Scarborough near the sea and loved walking along the seafront as often as she could. She felt she was more creative with her thinking and more connected to the universe when she could hear the waves and smell the sea. Once or twice she had met clients for a brisk seafront walk and coached them at the same time.

A niche was born. Together we decided that the majority of her coaching would take place on walks by the sea with her clients. Since most of her clients were based within a 10-mile radius of where she lived, Stephanie began advertising herself as 'The Seafront Coach'. The idea took off. On cold blustery days or when it rained they would use the shelters along the beach and no one seemed to mind being wrapped up against the elements. Stephanie said that people were more open and expressive when exposed to nature, and all her clients reported how much better they felt after their walks and her coaching.

Stephanie found a way of combining what she does best with what she loves to do. Her passion and enthusiasm for her unusual style of working were contagious and she maintains a regular client base, and is referred regularly by her satisfied 'walkers'.

First Steps

The road ahead may be a long one, but it starts with that very first step. By setting a date to begin, telling someone about it and then following through, you will be in the top two per cent of people who 'do it' rather than 'talk about it'. Everything I have ever achieved started with a commitment to taking that first step. You are no different.

Perhaps you now realize that you are not willing to do what it takes to do the work you first thought you would like to do. That's good to know, because it means that this is not your dream. Perhaps it was someone else's fantasy for you. Perhaps you thought this was what you 'should' do. I'm here to tell you to stop 'should-ing' all over yourself and create your own vision for the future, one that honours your unique talents and allows you to become who you want to be. Go back and do the exercise again. This time dream big. Ask yourself:

- What would I do if I knew I could not fail?
- What would I do if didn't have to earn another penny and I could do it all for free?

Fill in each definition once again and see what happens. You now have a blank canvas to draw on, so be bold.

Keeping the Dream Alive

The last and most important part of the exercise for me is the question 'What would happen if you didn't at least try to achieve your Ultimate Ideal Career?' I coach so many people who tell me that they never chose their career. Instead they were told what to do, or knew what they were expected to do. For my part, I had always wanted to be a journalist. In those days my parents thought it much safer for me to become a shorthand typist. They had their reasons, all of them to keep me secure, I don't doubt. However, I never lost the dream. Now I am able to write and coach and do pretty much what every journalist does under a different title.

There is a wonderful quote by Anaïs Nin which says, 'And the day came when the risk to remain tight in a bud was more painful than the risk it took to blossom.' Is your Ultimate Ideal Career path compelling? Is it an absolute Must Have? Would you regret it for years to come if you didn't do it? Yes? Then it's your turn to blossom. Go for it!

The truth is that living life according to your own values, and putting those values into action, is a radical act. Not everyone will agree or support your choices. You may have concerned friends and family tell you to get a 'proper job'. They have their own agenda. You have a choice: either let their voices drown you out or play your music louder.

Your Operating Instructions

Earlier on I said that you would have an opportunity to look at all the areas of your life and create your own rules or values for each area. So now, using the same template, take the following areas:

- Health
- Family
- Friends
- Fun and recreation
- Money
- Spirituality/religion/personal development.

Use the definitions to create your own set of operating instructions for your life.

Once you have a comprehensive list, you can begin to think about designing your own life purpose statement.

A great life purpose statement is an expression of

a) Your values – what's most important to you
b) Your vision – what you want to see happen in your life and the lives of those around you
c) Actions – the methods and actions you take to create your desired outcome.

Having a life purpose statement gives you a hook on which to hang your life. It doesn't mean that you are defined by it. We are all so much more than what we say we do. This is much more about *who you want to be* this time around. Having an underlying purpose gives life meaning.

Here are a couple of examples of what a life purpose statement looks like and how to create your own.

Francine's Life Purpose Statement
'I am a catalyst so that people can uncover their truth.'

You can see that my statement is very short but it does what it says on the tin. My purpose is to be present for that moment in time that people spend with me, whether as clients, family or friends, where through our communication something happens which allows them to see their life issues at the level of what is true for them. It's not as if I do this with everyone all the time. I do this where and when appropriate, using my intuition to let me know when the time is right and with others' permission to speak on a deeper level.

Here's another example. I have broken it down to give you an idea of how to construct your own statement. You could use this kind of structure or just keep it very simple like mine.

'The YMCA of San Francisco, based in Judeo-Christian heritage [values/core ideology] seeks to enhance the lives of all people [vision/

purpose] through programmes designed to develop spirit, mind and body [mission/methods/activity].'

Creating a Vision Board

Your mission, should you choose to accept it, is to take some time to think about what your life purpose is. To help you do this, you need to create a Vision Board.

Cut out pictures that represent the kind of life you want to live. Maybe there's the boat you want to own. Perhaps the house with land, the cottage by the sea, a picture of the type of person you want to spend your life with; literally anything that inspires you. Notice which of your values the pictures honour for you.

Once you have your Vision Board, create your life purpose statement. Put it up somewhere you can see it every day. Every morning take a look at your board and your statement; if it still fits the bill after 30 days, you have probably got it spot on. If not, keep tweaking it until it does.

Armed with your new set of operating instructions, you now know your values and have an idea of your vision and the actions you need to take to live a life that inspires you. You are well on the way to living your new life your way.

The Divorce Doctor's Personal Prescription for Taking Charge of Your Career: Five-day Treatment

Directions for Use

You are required to create your own rules for your life based on your personal values. This is the foundation from which to create a vision that inspires and motivates you to do work that fulfils your purpose in life.

Dosage

1. At the end of each day for the next 30 days, ask yourself 'Which of my values did I honour today and how did I do that?'

2. At the beginning of each day for the next 30 days, take five minutes and look at your vision board, then close your eyes and imagine that you already have everything pictured. Experience what it feels like to have it all. See yourself living out your dreams. Hear the sounds around you, smell the smell of success, contentment and fulfilment, really observe yourself living this life.

3. In 30 days' time, write down what effects this exercise has had on your life.

Self-affirmation Medicine

The following affirmations must be repeated at least three times each, three times per day for five consecutive days:

*   I have a vision of my fabulous future and can see myself living it every day.

*   Today I am free to define and live my life in alignment with my values.

*   Today I will choose from heart and trust my intuition to guide me.

Chapter 8
Having a Healthy Balance – Making More Time for Your Life

Awareness	Of where your time is going
Attitude	How you choose to spend your time
Action	What you need to do to make more time for your life

'I've had a wonderful time, but this wasn't it.' - **Groucho Marx**

Isn't that the truth? This is a quote I dined out on for many months after my divorce. Right now you have so many things going on in your life that it's hard to find time to breathe, but if you don't find a way to balance the time in your life you will become stressed and it will have an impact on your overall health.

A balanced life looks different for everyone, but in general it means getting the important stuff done, feeling fulfilled rather than feeling like you are on a hamster wheel, and having at least a little time for yourself.

In order to have a healthy relationship with time, it helps to make some distinctions. Some people have been out of balance for so long they cannot imagine living any other way. I'm going to show you how imbalance occurs, the reasons behind it and what you can do to regain your equilibrium.

Balanced Time

Let's get physical. I want you to *experience* a feeling of imbalance and its results. Yes, I can hear you say that you already feel that way! So let me show you how to sum up 'headless chicken' in an exercise I run in most of my seminars. It will give you a powerful illustration of what's going on in your life.

> Find a safe place to stand with plenty of space around you.
> From this position, stretch your arms out wide. In the same
> position stand on tiptoe. OK, now really stand on tiptoe.
> Now stand on tiptoe on one leg.

What happened? Did you lose your balance? Did you try to compensate by grabbing hold of something? What did you do to stay balanced?

When we are out of balance in any area of our lives, we feel out of control. Some people regain their balance by reaching out to someone else (or several someone elses) to tell their problems to, or to food, alcohol, cigarettes, sleep, drugs or TV. Many of us look for quick fixes to help us regain balance at any cost so that we can get back in control of our lives. When we perceive we are really losing control, we call it stress and become so overwhelmed that we either stumble around on automatic pilot or we simply crumble. If this is where your life is heading right now, you need to become aware of your most acute stress points so that you can make some immediate changes.

Stressed Time

My definition of stress is doing too much of what makes you most uncomfortable. When you do this repeatedly, there will be mental and physical reactions. The cycle works like this:

You are doing too much of what makes you uncomfortable. This could be overworking, trying to fit far too much into your day, caring for too many people, or whatever it is for you. You feel drained of energy, your resistance is lowered, your immune system is under pressure, your judgement and performance are impaired, you are less happy, less self-confident and ultimately under this amount of pressure you could break down mentally and physically. We all know someone who has suffered in this way and I don't want to it to be you.

'It's Never the Situation ...'

A clue to understanding what causes your stress on a daily basis lies in the emotions you experience beneath the surface of stress. You'll remember that earlier I said that *it's never the person, the situation or the circumstance that will ever frustrate or upset; it's always the* **value** *of yours that has been dishonoured or violated.* Well, it's the same with stress. It's not specifically the person, the situation or the circumstance that is stressing you out, it's the value of yours that is not being honoured and it shows up via an emotional reaction which can be so powerful that it hides the real reason for your stress from yourself and those around you. Let me show you what I mean.

Cheryl and Haydn divorced because Haydn was abusive mentally and, on several occasions, physically. Cheryl left Haydn with just the clothes she and the children (aged four and seven) were wearing. She had to camp outside the social services offices with her kids until they opened in the morning, and luckily she received bed and breakfast accommodation that very same night. For the next nine months they shared one room until Cheryl managed to secure a council flat on an estate which had a reputation for being rough. She desperately wanted to go back to work, not only to support her kids but for her own self-esteem.

Cheryl had several main areas of stress to deal with, and as a result her prevalent mood each day was short tempered and anxious.

The first area of stress was maintaining security and safety where she lived and avoiding her ex-husband. The second was childcare so she could work, the third was money and the fourth was making sure her children were protected from 'bad' outside influences.

I helped Cheryl to discover the emotion underneath her stress. Together we discovered that it was the fear that ultimately her children would be taken away from her. Underneath *that* stress was something similar – the fear that she would become ill and her children would lose her. Her stress was understandable and totally valid, but in fact was self-defeating and working against her. All Cheryl's time, without exception, was spent in this state. If she carried on in this cycle of panic and stress it was entirely possible that her worst fears would become reality.

We had to get into action and the first thing we had to do was look at her options for resolving her stress. We took out pen and paper and started writing. The first point was safety and security. This was Cheryl's number-one value. We arranged that Cheryl would get in touch with her local crime prevention officer at the police station and ask for advice on how to stay safe inside and outside her home. They were very helpful and let Cheryl know how she could get proper locks on her front door and secure her home for a minimum cost. Cheryl got a personal alarm which she kept with her when taking the kids in and out of the flats and surrounding area, and felt immediately more relaxed that she could at least do something if she felt in danger. She also enrolled herself and the kids into a martial arts class which was run for free in a nearby school. They all went together after school and had fun practising at home. This was great exercise for her and the children, and as they progressed Cheryl could see the children grow in confidence. She began to feel her fears around their safety at school decrease.

Next Cheryl found a part-time job as a cleaner in a nearby residential home. It wasn't her first choice of job but, as someone once said to me, 'If you want a job, get a job, *any* job.' Once you are in work, it's much easier to move to another job. Cheryl fitted her cleaning job in with the children's school hours, which worked well. After five weeks of getting into action in her life she was ready to address creating space and time for herself. A small group of women on the estate had created an afternoon club on a Sunday in the local community hall. The idea was that each week a couple of mums would have from 12 to 6 p.m. off knowing their kids were being well looked after. This only happened once a month, but this one afternoon was Cheryl's lifeline. This was her thinking and planning time, and we decided that each month she would create a goal for the month ahead based on her values and her vision for her future.

By month three Cheryl had decided to become a care worker in the residential home where she cleaned. Cheryl felt more fulfilled caring for the elderly residents. Cheryl still experienced the normal everyday stresses of running out of milk for cereal, the kids being late for school and making the money stretch to the end of the month, but she was beginning to feel more in control of her life, and more in control of her children's security and safety. Her stress had turned into the usual everyday concerns, which she knew she could handle.

Here are some questions I would like you to ask yourself about the stress in your life:

- What issue or issues are causing you stress?
- What emotion is underneath that stress?
- Is there any other concern underneath that?
- What's the worst thing that could happen?

When you've had a careful think about what's underneath your stress, you're in a much better position to resolve (or at least lessen) it. Think about your own strengths and resources, and how you can bring these to your aid in improving the situation causing you stress. What are your options for resolving your stress? Who can offer you practical advice?

Emotional Time

Time is an emotional business. Think of an instance when you had to do some mundane chore or repetitive task. How did you feel? Did you procrastinate and put it off until the last minute? Then when you did it did you feel resentful, irritated or just plain bored? Ever notice how something that could be done in a very short time takes far longer than it should because you become so distracted by other things, so that you end up late for something else? Look how many negative emotions are involved in something you don't really want to do.

Now think of a time when you were having fun. Didn't time just fly?

So time is about emotions. We can't always do what we enjoy 24/7. I don't enjoy dragging heavy dustbins up and down my driveway, but when I miss out on a week's collection just because I've 'forgotten' it was Thursday, the consequence of piled-up rubbish evokes an emotion of disgust far greater than the inconvenience of making sure I get the bins ready.

Emotional Control

Recognizing your emotions as you approach each task during your day gives you back your control over time. Taking control of your emotions and making choices based on how you will feel if you do or don't do a task helps you to make distinctions about where to focus your time. It's also a far healthier approach than allowing your emotions free rein without understanding what they are trying to tell you.

Make a short list of everything you don't enjoy having to do in your life right now, and the emotions that go along with this. For example:

Task	Emotion
Taking out the bins	Resentment that I have to do it
Doing the shopping	Tiredness and panic that it takes up time I could be spending elsewhere
Sending out invoices	Frustration with admin tasks I hate

Now make a list of what you *do* enjoy doing.

Task	Emotion
Cooking dinner for my kids	Warmth and pleasure of providing them with a meal and spending time together
Being creative at work	Fulfilment, satisfaction, pleasure
Paying my bills on time	Freedom, peace of mind, being in control

Get the picture? When people tell me that they find it difficult to manage their own time, that they spend most of their waking hours in a state of anxiety or they haven't time to do something important, I know that we need to look at what each task *means* to them and how it affects them emotionally.

Valued Time

It's amazing how important it is to feel good about anything we spend our time doing for ourselves and others. Because time is such an emotional issue, it helps to become conscious of why we no longer feel we have time to do something we used to enjoy.

I had a client whose wife liked him to make her a cup of coffee each morning before he left for work. He used to enjoy doing that for her; it was one way of showing her his love. Over the years, though, she stopped thanking him for it. He felt taken for granted and began to look at what he was getting back in return. He decided that he no longer had the *time* to make her coffee. She felt that he didn't care about her any more, and a battle continued for the next two years because a husband felt unappreciated and basically unloved but didn't tell his wife the real reason. Instead he just withdrew his services. I pointed out that it was actually his value of appreciation that had been trodden on, and on that note we began our work together.

Where Is Your Time Going?

Over the next few days I'd like you to put your time 'under observation'. Some clients keep a time log of what they do in a day, with comments by the side. It may sound like yet another thing to do, but it will give you a clear picture of where your physical and emotional time is being spent. Here's a time log I prepared back in 1998 when I was creating time-management seminars.

TASK	Date	TIME TAKEN	Comments
Jotting down notes for workshop	14/6/98	45 mins	Very exciting to start!
Trying to plan the workshop	19/6/98	procrastinated for two days = approx 14 hours!	Confusing and I don't know how to go about it. Scared it won't work.
Preparing one module	21/6/98	4 hours	A struggle, but more satisfying
Presenting workshop	27/6/98	4 hours	Exhilarating!

One year later I had to create another workshop.

TASK	Date	TIME TAKEN	Comments
Doing notes for workshop with Susan	10/7/99	10 minutes	Very exciting and confidence building
Planning the workshop	10/7/99	10 minutes with Susan	Happy, and still excited rather than anxious
Preparing one module	11/7/99	30 minutes with 10-minute call to Susan	Satisfied and proud
Presenting workshop	15/7/99	4 hours	Calm, relaxed and very connected. Feeling great

The difference was obviously asking Susan for help. But Susan didn't do it for me. She asked me to close my eyes and tell me exactly what I wanted the people at the workshop to receive, what the purpose of that was and what strategies and actions I wanted them to take to achieve results. Within minutes we had notes for the whole workshop.

The workshop had four modules, so we broke it down into chunks and came up with four main headings. This took another 10 minutes. I went away to create a time-line for the modules and phoned Susan for her opinion on the order of certain strategies. I completed Module 1 in 40 minutes.

With my fearful emotions out of the way I was able to ask for help from the perfect source and complete the task in 1 hour instead of 22 hours and 45 minutes!

Changing Your Emotion

In order to get anything done, you need to separate the emotion from the task, *or* associate the task with a different emotion. Don't ever be afraid to ask for help with this. You are not an island and two heads are better than one. You can ask your kids, your friends, work colleagues, family, even a neighbour. Be direct and don't waffle. Come to the point, ask for help and stick to the task at hand. Remember to return the favour when they next need some help and you should always have a ready supply of willing supporters.

Going It Alone

If you haven't a soul to help you and there are tasks that you cannot avoid doing, you'll have to practise self-help. Ask yourself,

- What do I currently feel about this task?
- In order to feel differently, what perspective do I need to look at it from?

Never-ending Lists and How to Handle Them

I don't want to give you any more 'to do lists' than you already have. What I'd like is to give you some simple strategies to help you minimize your lists. The truth is the only time the list is complete is when they finally put the lid down and you return to your maker. Life is an eternal list – and thank goodness for that. Life would be so boring otherwise. So, go ahead and make as many lists as you want – but as you do, ask yourself:

Does it need to be done today? This week? This month?

These are the three magic rules of time which will allow you to take the pressure off wherever you can. You must be completely honest, though. Is it absolutely vital to get it done today? What would happen if you didn't get it done today? Would you lose your home, your job, your kids or the cat? Would your life crumble around you? Probably not.

The trick is to get the important stuff done and still have time for you. To help you focus on what's most important every day, I am going to arm you with two great tools to help you. First off, you need an understanding of the 20/80 principle.

20/80 Time

The fact is that only a small percentage of our input produces the majority of results. This is called *the Pareto Principle*. Vilfredo Pareto was an Italian economist who, around 1900, studied the distribution of wealth in Italy. He discovered a common phenomenon: a consistent minority – about 20 per cent of the people – controlled about 80 per cent of the wealth. Pareto called this a 'predictable imbalance'. This plays itself out in sales – 80 per cent of your income comes from 20 per cent of your customers – and in the workplace, where 80 per cent of your problems arise from 20 per cent of your staff.

Right now in your life, 80 per cent of your challenges probably come from the one person who makes up only 20 per cent of your life. (No prizes for guessing who!) When I pointed out to a harassed client planning her second wedding that 80 per cent of her seating-plan problems were coming from 20 per cent of her guests, she was surprised that this was almost exactly correct.

However long your 'to do list', only 20 per cent of that list is absolutely vital. This is great news, because once you have accomplished that 20 per cent you have the rest of the day to do what you want with. Part of the remaining 80 per cent can be rescheduled for a time when it really needs to be done, and part of it can happen spontaneously when you feel like doing it.

Most people will find that on a daily basis there are probably two or three tasks that simply have to be done. For me it was taking the kids to school, going to work and making dinner. They were my basics. In between there were tasks like paying my car tax, dentist appointments and keeping my studies going, etc. I put these into my diary on the relevant days and they became part of my vital 20 per cent for *that* day. One client said that much of his 20 per cent took place at work, but getting specific tasks out of the way relaxed him so much that he got far more done outside work because he was calmer.

Your Time Audit

Take your own time audit to find out how you currently manage your time.

Read the statements shown below and select a letter that most closely matches your own response. When you're done, add up your total number of As, Bs Cs or Ds.

A = Never

B = Sometimes

C = Mostly

D = Always

1. I find myself taking on various jobs because I'm the only one who can do them.
2. I transfer so many 'to do' items to the next day that I feel like I haven't accomplished anything.
3. I get distracted easily. I start something and leave it unfinished.
4. I'm forgetful about appointments, deadlines and personal commitments.
5. I suffer from tiredness, with lots of unproductive time.
6. I find it difficult to get myself organized.
7. I feel guilty that I don't spend enough quality time with my family and friends.
8. I make plans for the future but I don't follow through.
9. I don't have time to exercise regularly and I eat packaged or takeaway food.
10. I tend to keep putting things off.
11. I'm frustrated by the slowness of people and things around me; I hate to wait or stand in a queue.
12. I keep thinking that one day I'll be able to do what I really want to do.

Mostly A

Congratulations, you know exactly how to make time work for you. You are organized, focused and spend your time wisely. I imagine you have a comfortable work/life balance and have plenty of time to pursue your hobbies and spend quality time with family and friends. You are probably healthy and fit, and this makes you an example to us all.

Because you are so good at managing your time, you may want to offer support to those around you struggling to manage their time. However, rather than telling them what they *should* be doing, let people know what works for you and leave them to decide whether to try out your strategies. When they can see how well you are managing your time, it's likely that they will want to find out exactly how you do it.

Mostly B

Well done. You have the basic knowledge and skills to manage your time, and most of the time you get great results. However, there is room for continued vigilance. You now need to make sure that your time is invested wisely. To do this, you must develop a more conscious attitude about how you spend your time.

Mostly C

This is disappointing. You have been wasting a great deal of your time, and your energy, vitality and health are probably suffering as a result. You are a few steps away from losing track of time.

Time wasted today cannot be rolled over until tomorrow. Use it or lose it. You need to get back to basics. You are probably taking on far too much because you don't believe anyone can do the job as well as you, or tell yourself that it's far quicker to do it yourself. This means that you feel responsible for everything. You probably feel overwhelmed, which leads to disorganization and to frustration when hours and days slip by with little accomplished. This is a dangerous downward spiral.

You are not an island and you need to accept some support to help you get organized and back on track. It's impossible to do everything yourself. Take the risk of trusting others for the pay-off of having more time for yourself and what you choose to do. It really is worth it.

Take a good look at your health. Are you eating well? Are you taking exercise or are you spending hours in front of the TV with snacks and fizzy drinks? Tiredness, lack of motivation, impatience and mental apathy are signs of an unfulfilled life and this needs to be addressed.

Time means little if we live unhealthy lives. Get some good nutritional advice from your doctor and start exercising. Just a 20-minute brisk walk each day will change your mood, give you more energy and is a great start to revitalizing your life. Once you are feeling more alert and your energy levels rise, you will be more able to address the real changes that you need to make. Get your trainers out and get moving, you have no more time to waste.

Mostly D

Unfortunately you have lost the plot when it comes to managing the time in your life. This time audit is long overdue. In order to make up for lost time you need to take a long and honest look at your life. It would appear that you are overwhelmed and probably not doing anything that satisfies or fulfils you. You need to take a full inventory of your life. A great many changes need to take place because your time bank is running on empty.

Below are some ways for you to take the first steps towards reinvesting time in yourself and your life.

Saying Yes to Something Means Saying No to Something Else

You only have so much time in your time bank on a daily basis. Get really conscious about what you say 'yes' to, because it could mean that you are saying 'no' to other things of importance to you, like time to exercise or spend with friends and family.

People make up all sorts of reasons why they can't say no. They don't want to appear difficult or selfish or be thought badly of. However, if you compromise your own needs over and over again, it will only lead to poor health in the end. Learn to say no and be honest enough to give your reasons. After my divorce I actually decided not to see some people whom I realized I had nothing in common with any more. It was difficult to turn down kind invitations, but I thanked them and explained that I was in a different place and needed time to find my feet. This freed me up to build new friendships and include people in my life who were more in alignment with my lifestyle.

It's a good idea to create some strong personal boundaries that you do not compromise; otherwise you will find yourself wasting some of your precious time doing things out of duty when you could be doing more of what makes you happy.

Outcome/purpose/action – the Power of Focus

I love learning from successful people, and one thing I have learned is that the people who get the most value from their time know how to focus on three things:

1. They know what they want
2. They know why they want it
3. They know the right actions to take that will achieve their desired outcome.

On a daily basis before you do anything, ask yourself:

- What do I want? What am I trying to achieve?
- Why do I want it? What will it provide me with when I get it? What purpose will it serve?
- What do I need to do to get it?

It's much easier to decide what to do and create an action plan when you are first clear about your outcome. It's great to be spontaneous some of the time, but during and after divorce your life may already resemble a juggling act. If you know the outcome you wish to achieve and stay focused on that, you can get the job done with time to spare.

Anticipated Time

Another powerful tool to add to your toolkit is the power of anticipation. Whilst it is impossible to work out what might happen and how you will handle it, at least anticipating the consequences of your actions to some degree will stop the rug being pulled out from under you as vigorously as it might be. My grandmother used to say, 'Francine, think before you speak.' I was always a 'say it as it is' type of girl, but her simple advice has served me exceptionally well over the years. In this case, I'd like you to 'anticipate before you take action'. If you at least have an idea of how others might react, what might happen if you take action and what might happen if you don't, you have a plan B in place that could save you hours of regret.

Failing to Plan Is Planning to Fail

I cannot urge you enough to plan, plan and plan again. Planning is the tool that will keep you on track to achieving the results you need from your day. Consistent daily planning will allow you to get everything done and feel like you are controlling your time rather than the other way round.

Here's how you do it.

- Take a look at your week and write down a 'wish list' of everything you want to get done that week.
- Look at each item. Ask yourself the magic question 'Does this need to be done today, this week or this month?' Be honest. It's not possible to do a whole week's work in one day. Some tasks will have deadlines and some will not.
- Put all your 'this weeks' and 'this months' in your diary or organizer on the appropriate dates when they'll need your attention.
- Prioritize your 'today' items by deciding which 20 per cent are absolutely vital. Your 20 per cent items will typically have a deadline, or will be of such importance that they will supersede everything else.

Planning your time in this way will reap great benefits.

Your Time Satisfaction Scale

On a scale of 1 to 10 (1 being 'not at all' satisfied and 10 being 'totally'), score your satisfaction with the amount of time you are able to spend on each of these areas of your life:

- Family and friends
- Career
- Fun and recreation
- Money
- Personal growth
- Significant other (partner or spouse)
- Environment (where you live)
- Health.

If any of these ranks below a 7, ask yourself 'What would I have to do in order to raise the score to an 8?' The answer will point you towards what you need to do to take back control of your life and your time.

Making Choices

> *'Some people make things happen. Some people watch things happen. Some people say "What happened?"'* **– Gaelic proverb**

I love this proverb. All of us have done all three at one time or another, but now you really do have the power to choose to take control of your life and decide how you will respond to all the stuff that happens each day. Your response will dictate what you do next to make the things happen that will bring harmony, balance and happiness back into your life.

Your language is also an important tool. Using the words 'I choose' puts you in control of your time rather than firefighting through it.

So what will you choose to do with your time after divorce? I hope that one of the things you will do is ....

Take Time for Pleasure

Ah, pleasure! I could not end this chapter without including some thoughts about making time for pleasure. There has been a great deal of turmoil and heart-wrenching emotions to deal with; part of moving towards life after divorce is finding out what makes you happy.

Your interests add richness to life, and without them you will swap your soul for an eternal treadmill of work, kids and chores. It's time to be more selfish. Find time for you, because you can't share yourself unless you have a self to share.

Physical Break Time

We all need to schedule in physical breaks. There is no point waiting until your body gives up on you – by then it's too late. Do whatever it takes to have a couple of weekends at least during the year, without the family, to simply be you. You don't even have to share this time with friends. A client took a few days in the midst of her divorce to go to her favourite place in the sun. She read books and swam during the day, ate lunch on the terrace of her hotel by the sea, and in the evening had her evening meal under the stars before going to bed at a reasonable time to luxuriate in crisp sheets and a double bed all to herself. After just two days she felt totally rejuvenated and ready to face the world again. How wonderful does that sound?

The point is that you must look after your body – it's the only one you have. If you take care of it, it will repay you by giving you the valuable energy you need.

The Time Is Now

With all this talk about forward planning, anticipating where possible and scheduling your priorities, it's important to remember that you can only live from moment to moment. The past is over, the future isn't here yet; we only ever have the present moment in which to live.

Nature doesn't run by the clock. Trees don't know what time is, nor do rivers nor flowers nor seas. In nature there is only now, and that's true for us too. The trick to managing your time is learning to focus in the here and now.

Right now, stop and just look around you. Notice where you are, notice what's around you, feel your body on the chair you are sitting on, notice if your eyes are dry or moist, wiggle your fingers and stretch out your toes. Release your neck and take a deep breath. Welcome to the present.

It's useful to stop like this several times during your busy day just to check in with yourself. Whilst you are having a shower, take a moment to feel the water on your body; when you arrive home, experience the relief of taking off your shoes and letting the day go. As you hug your kids, take an extra moment to experience how good it feels. How many times have you driven to work or the shops and not even noticed the journey? Take time at the traffic lights to *be present*.

Don't let life just pass you by whilst you are on your way to the next activity. The time is now, so stay as present as you can to all of it.

Personal Prescription for Making Time for Your Life: Five-day Observation Treatment

Directions for Use

You are required to observe where your time goes each day. For at least two days, keep a time log so that you are clear about what you are doing, how long it takes and whether the time spent produces specific outcomes. Notice where you waste time doing things that don't produce outcomes that enrich your life, and become more aware of what you can control and what changes you can make.

Dosage

Each morning set yourself a 'positive intention' for the day ahead. For example:

- Today I will walk in the fresh air for 15 minutes.
- Today I will leave work on time.
- Today I will choose to be everywhere I need to be on time.

Repeat your positive intention three times during the day.

Self-affirmation Medicine

The following affirmations must be repeated three times per day each, and added to your affirmation list.

- I am fully present in my life.
- There is enough time to do what I need to do.
- I am always in control of the time in my life.

Part 4
The Recovery Room

Chapter 9
From Conflict to Co-operation

Awareness	That the past does not equal the future
Attitude	Being able to accept and forgive
Action	Doing what you need to do to move from conflict to co-operation

'The past is another country; they do things differently there.' **- L P Hartley**

Hurray! Your old relationship is now behind you and it's time to move on with your life and get yourself to a place where you can use your past to learn from. It's time to start letting go and, as you take the first steps towards recuperation and recovery from what has been a long and emotional journey, it's *definitely* time to understand that your past does not equal your future – unless you allow it to.

Back there in the past, you and you partner did what you did and said what you said with the resources you had available to you both at the time. If either of you could have done it differently, you would have done. The truth is, neither of you knew any other way. There is no blame, just behaviours that were not acceptable to you and personal values of yours that you were not able to honour in your relationship with your ex. Now, because you understand how your relationship inevitably ended up where it did, you have a new set of resources to work with. So are you ready to embrace the fact that the past is another country and you simply don't live there any more?

A Healthy Perspective – a Gift in the Garbage

I won't lie, it's not like you are ever going to forget what has happened. In fact, I wouldn't want you to. Instead, I would suggest that everything that happened during your relationship had a reason, and that reason was to get you to where you are right now.

I would also suggest that there is another perspective, which is that your partnership with your ex was arguably one of the greatest gifts in your life. I'm not joking. Yes, I know that if you are still in financial warfare or child-contact battles this is not the way you view your relationship right now. However, I'd like you to consider the possibility that there is 'a gift in the garbage' as a client so elegantly put it when describing what she had learned from her ex. You would not be the person you are growing into without having had this experience in your life. I know it seems like one you could well have done without, but I promise you that as you look back on your life you will understand that this had to happen in order for you to become who you will be.

There is no such thing as coincidence; just people, circumstances and incidents that coincide on your path of life. All of them, without question, arrive at exactly the right time to teach you what you need to learn. I have spoken to hundreds of men and women who have travelled the same path you are on right now. Every one of them found a gift in their garbage, and all of them, without exception, have grown emotionally and spiritually from their experience.

My wish is that this chapter may give you a new perspective from which to view your time together and see it as the special gift it has been – and use it to understand yourself and how you operate in a relationship. If you can do this you will be able to move forward into your new life from a place of compassion and understanding for the people both you *and* your ex have been – because the truth is that neither of you could have done it any other way.

Jerry had been married to Barbara for 14 years. When they first met, Barbara had been a quiet girl but very caring and loving towards Jerry. Jerry had lost both his parents within months of each other when he was 12. They had been on a business trip (he'd stayed with his grandmother while they were away), and they had caught malaria and died shortly afterwards. He had visited them when they had been transferred to hospital in England, and he remembers feeling so helpless, like he should have done something to save them but couldn't.

It was incredibly painful to lose both parents and, at 12 years old, Jerry made up his mind that he should have known what to do to save them, even though he was reassured that there was nothing he could have done. He went to live with his grandmother, who was already 72 at the time and not well herself. Five years later, Jerry found himself looking after her until she died when he was 19. Meeting Barbara at university two years later he was immediately attracted to her gentle ways, which brought out his protective nature. There was something fragile about her and he just wanted to take care of her.

Barbara had experienced a difficult childhood. Her mother was depressed most of the time and spent days in bed, and her father worked as a long-distance lorry driver and was rarely home. As a result her mother developed a possessive relationship with Barbara. University was her escape route and one that her mother actually urged her to take, but Barbara still rang her mother twice a day to make sure she was OK, and spent most of her time feeling guilty that she was not home caring for her. In her last term at university, her mother took an overdose of her tablets, fell asleep and did not wake up. Barbara was filled with overpowering guilt and grief. Jerry tried to do everything he could to console her. He could imagine how she felt and had so much compassion for her.

Barbara's need for Jerry grew and it was matched by his need to protect her. They married shortly after they left university and lived in a bedsit until they both had jobs and began to move up the ladder of life. But Barbara never seemed happy and would become withdrawn for weeks at a time. Jerry thought that she was still grieving over her mother and urged her to get some help for any unresolved issues around this. Barbara refused because she was so afraid that she was turning into her mother. This left Jerry in a dilemma. He did not know what to do to help and could not *make* her go and see someone.

On top of this, after they had been married for three years Barbara decided that she did not want to have children. This made Jerry really sad. If Barbara had been happy with their lives together, he would have been prepared to accept this. But she wasn't. After 12 years of trying every strategy he could think of to make Barbara happy, without any major result, he became ill himself. He caught bronchitis, which turned into pneumonia. It was so bad that he was hospitalized. Barbara fell apart. She did not know what to do. She didn't know how to support him because she had been the supported one; she didn't visit him in hospital and sank into a depression.

This was a turning point for Jerry. The one time he had needed Barbara she had fallen to pieces. He realized that the only person he had never looked after was himself. He spent his recovery period doing some hard thinking. After he got well, he asked Barbara for a divorce. He decided that he had no more strategies left in him and knew that he could never make Barbara happy. He realized that he didn't even remember the last time he had laughed or had anything back from Barbara that he could describe as happiness, and he had nothing left to give. Their divorce was very upsetting until the day the *decree nisi* arrived. At first Jerry felt a sense of relief and liberation. But three months later, he called me sounding distraught and said that he was finding it terribly difficult to let go, recuperate from the pain of divorce and experience his own recovery.

There had been a great many losses in Jerry's life. First there was the loss of both his parents and then the loss of his grandmother. Now Barbara. His divorce had brought back all the sadness around his parents dying and losing his grandmother. It seemed there was nothing he could do to hold on to the people that he loved, and he figured that the common denominator in all of these losses was himself. Because he had been unable to help Barbara, he was once again experiencing the familiar feelings of helplessness he'd first known as a child. He was experiencing loss on top of loss and was unable to figure a way out. Thankfully he had asked for help.

When we first met, Jerry was confused. He was hurt and angry that the only time that he had needed Barbara she was not there for him, after he had been there for her for so many years. On the other hand, the voice in his head told him that he should have been able to save his relationship with her. He struggled with the thoughts that he was so right about how wrong Barbara had been to have behaved the way she did, but he allowed me to suggest that perhaps neither of them was to blame. Isn't it possible, I asked, that they were both just doing the best they could with the resources they had available to them at the time? Could either of them have behaved any differently? I didn't think so.

This is something I will reiterate throughout this chapter because I really want you to hear it: *if they could have done it differently they would, but they were doing the best they could given the personal resources they both had available at the time.*

Understanding this is the key to moving from conflict to co-operation, and unlocks the door of your new life and your full recovery from your divorce.

Barbara did not set out to make Jerry's life difficult any more than Jerry wanted to hurt Barbara. It's that simple. Exactly the same applies to you and your relationship. Whatever you have given and whatever you have received in return, under any and in every circumstance good and bad, it's only with hindsight that you can be clever enough to look back in judgement. At the time you made the only choices you could. If you could have done it any differently, you would have done.

Letting Go

OK, so how long does it take to recover fully and let go?

The answer is that while the decision to let go can happen in an instant, for most people it doesn't happen overnight and the amount of time it takes is different for everyone.

Letting go is an emotional process, and people make the process even harder by attaching so many meanings to it. One of the reasons why it is so hard to let go is that it can feel like saying goodbye to both a familiar past and a dreamed-of future. You are launching yourself into an unknown place, somewhere you have never lived before and that may look pretty scary from where you are right now. Another reason why it's so hard to let go is that you have no idea *who* you will be without your old ways of being. Jerry, for example, had no idea who he would be without someone to help in his life. He had structured his life around caring for someone.

Many of us structure our lives according to our old wiring, and think that if we are not living in a certain way we will lose our identity. This is not the truth. In order to heal your own life you have to be able to free yourself from all the old excuses that have kept you from looking at yourself. If you use anyone or anything as a reason to keep you from taking the time to know yourself and be true to yourself, you just move further away from the special gift that is being offered to you right now.

The Hidden Gift

Jerry had been playing out his 'old wiring' in relationship with Barbara. 'I have to help' was what he decided he had to do after his parents died. But he could not help Barbara because she needed to put her own demons to bed. Actually, helping her had the effect of allowing her to stay stuck in her old patterns. Jerry was unwittingly colluding with Barbara to maintain her old pattern of behaviour. The hidden gift for Jerry was learning to examine his old ways of being in a relationship so that he now had a choice. Was he actually *projecting* his need to protect and help others onto Barbara because of his past? Was this more about *his* need to help rather than what Barbara really needed? Even if these were natural and not learned tendencies of his, how well did his strategy serve Barbara and, ultimately, their relationship? Wanting to help is a wonderful quality, but Jerry needed to make a clear distinction between satisfying his own needs and what Barbara might (or might not) benefit from.

Many of us have been so hard-wired that we believe deep in our hearts that we are being kind, unselfish and loving when really, at least in part, we are serving ourselves. If you can use the letting-go process to re-evaluate and reflect on your own behaviours honestly, the gift that appears will lead you towards a new way of being and a new, more positive, set of rules and boundaries for your life.

Letting Go of 'If Only'

Recovery is a time of release, and part of learning to let go is also about getting over the thought that things could have been different 'if only'. 'If only he'd listened,' 'If only she could change,' 'If only I'd known what was happening,' 'If only he could have been more of this and less of that.' Letting go means dropping 'if only' and accepting the other person the way he or she is. It's also about accepting yourself.

Let me show you what I mean.

Andrew's frustration with Sophie during their three-year marriage was that Sophie spent more time travelling abroad with her job as a photographer than she did at home with him. If only she had devoted more time to their relationship, which was good when they were together, he believed they would never have split up. When push came to shove, Sophie was not prepared to give up her job for the foreseeable future. At 26, this was her time to put into practice all she had learned and worked hard for. Andrew was 32 and wanted to start a family and have a more traditional family life. After their divorce, virtually every one of Andrew's sentences began with '*If only* ...' Our only route out was to ban him from using these words in our sessions together and replace them with 'What I now want is ...', which allowed Andrew to rediscover and take on board his own needs so that he could move forward and rebuild his life.

Just take a moment and think of an 'if only' about your relationship. For example 'If only he could have been honest with me that we were in debt, things would have been so different.' Are you any better off or any wiser for feeling this way? Has anything changed? 'If only' is a one-way street to nowhere. It's also incredibly boring for anyone else (even your long-suffering best friend) because you both know that it just wasn't that way. You can spend a lifetime 'if only-ing' and it won't make an iota of difference.

Letting Go of Being Right

Yet another part of the process is letting go of being right. This does not mean that you are condoning any behaviour that is unacceptable to you; it means that you are letting go of being right about how wrong your ex was for behaving the way they did. In their world they had a reason for doing what they did. If you asked them to explain themselves they would tell you that they acted that way because they believed they would get what they wanted for themselves. Holding on to being right about how wrong they were may allow you to justify your reasons for leaving or justify your anger and dislike. But it's a negative energy that will take up a lot of mind space and won't heal you or them.

The simple truth is that being with this person didn't work for you. Whether their behaviours work for someone else is not for you to judge. I had a client who had collected a consensus of opinion from *everyone* he knew about how wrong his wife was. He told me 'Everyone said that I was right, so I know that it isn't just me.' So what? You could get the whole of England to sign your 'justification of rightness' petition, but the fact is that your ex wasn't right for you and that's all there is to it. Ask yourself:

- What am I avoiding by holding on to being right?
- What don't I have to look at or confront when I am being right?
- Am I willing to face any of the above? Am I experiencing it anyway?

Be honest: which would you rather choose: holding on to the hurt of being right or allowing yourself to feel it and let it go? Letting go of being right releases its hold over you and gives you back your aliveness and clarity. When you have clarity you can move forward and do what needs to be done to get on with your life.

Letting Your Former Partner Go

Are you really willing to let your former partner go? You don't have to be happy about it, just willing. Try this exercise. I warn you that it can be a very emotional experience, so you have full permission to cry if you need to, but it will give you an idea of whether you are *willing* to let your former partner go.

> Sit down and imagine your former partner is sitting in the chair in front of you. Look into their eyes and say out loud 'I am willing to let you go. You have full permission to leave my life for ever.' Say it as many times as you need to until it feels like it's the truth.

How was that? Was it easier than you thought or much harder? Whatever your answer, it's an indicator of where you are right now in your process. If you want a bigger challenge, I suggest you tell the person to their face. Could you do that?

Forgiveness

Forgiveness is something that you are required to do if you truly want to move forward with your life. No two ways about it, people who are able to forgive have happier hearts than those who don't. But forgiveness is a subject all of its own, and because I believe in my own heart that it's not until you can forgive that you can truly love again, I am going to take this opportunity to explain forgiveness in detail so you can include it in your recovery process.

In my own life, if I had wanted to, I could also have gathered a consensus of opinion as to why I was right to end my marriage. No one would have argued with me, and I'll admit it felt good to hold on to my righteousness for a while. However, once the papers had been signed and my divorce was old news, I was left with a pain in my chest that would not go away. It erupted in angry telephone calls, low energy and a grumpiness that would not let up. It came out in words like 'It's not fair,' 'Poor me' and other victim language. It didn't sound like the 'me' I knew, and I wasn't behaving like the 'me' I now wanted to be, but I couldn't shake it off.

> I started to get really angry with myself because I didn't want to feel that way any more. Then a strange thing happened. I woke up one morning and decided that I was completely bored with being a victim. It hadn't got me anywhere except upset and in more pain, so in that moment I chose to forgive and let go. It happened in an instant and I couldn't quite believe it would last. But it did last. It was the most enormous relief. It felt like a weight had been lifted. I realized with some surprise that it had absolutely nothing to do with my ex-partner; he was still who he was. He didn't have to do anything; he was free to remain as he had always been. My circumstances had not changed, but *I* had changed. There were still difficult logistics with the kids and all the other stuff that parents apart have to deal with. There would still be Christmases and birthdays and high and holy days and it simply didn't make me feel sorry for myself any more. I no longer felt the need to hold on to any bad thoughts about my ex and, even more astonishing, bit by bit my compassion for my ex came back. I found I was able to talk to him and support him with the kids. I found I still cared about whether he was well or not. I found feelings of sadness over what could have been but probably would never have been, and I was still able to let go of being right about how wrong he was. I have never looked back. I have a distant but kind relationship with my ex. It serves my children well. I know he wishes me well and I wish him well, too.

I cannot express strongly enough how wonderful it is to forgive and let go. I know that you will get there in your own time, and that is the gold at the end of 'that there' tunnel. When it happens, your heart will have a lightness that will allow you to let love back in.

Forgiveness as a Concept

When I speak about forgiveness to clients, many find it a pretty challenging concept to get their heads round in the light of their experiences. So it may be helpful to explore the concept in more depth. A good place to start is with what forgiveness is *not*.

Forgiveness Is Not Forgetting

Forgiveness does not mean that you suddenly lose all memory of what happened during your relationship and develop amnesia over events that took place and experiences you've had. That would be neither realistic nor valuable. You cannot turn the clock back and erase your memories of hurt and unpleasantness in the past. Whether you like it or not, it happened.

However, you *can* change the way you think about the past so that it serves you as a place to learn from. Forgiveness in the context we are talking of here means freeing yourself and letting go. It means that you decide not to let the experiences of the past dictate your future and prevent you from being, doing or having everything that is possible for you. It's about *not allowing* your past memories to control your attitudes and behaviours in the present and the future.

But what about justice, you may ask? Well, there's legal justice and then there are situations where legal justice does not happen. You can kick and scream until you are out of breath and out of money. But unless you want to end up behind bars serving even more time for your ex, you can either wage your own private war or choose another way.

Forgiveness Is Not Condoning

I want to be very clear that forgiveness is not about absolving or condoning unacceptable behaviours that have affected you. I know that people have many reasons for their behaviours but they also have a responsibility for the choices that they make and the impact their choice of behaviour will have on other people. That why it's called 'free will'. Whilst you may argue in your own favour, if you look a little deeper I think you'll find that the *consequences* of some of your own behaviours, as well as those of your ex-partner, are playing themselves out in your divorce.

Forgiveness Does Not Invalidate Hurt

Forgiveness is not pretending that it didn't happen or that what happened wasn't such a big deal. If you have been hurt, you can't just brush it under the carpet and say it doesn't matter. It has to be dealt with. Forgiveness is not about making light of something which was fundamentally wrong.

Forgiveness Is Not Pretending

There is a distinction to be made between suppressing or denying your hurt and anger and truly forgiving. Once again, it's all in the 'letting go'. You are not asked to be a martyr; forgiveness is not about self-sacrifice. Smiling when you are just stuffing down your real feelings can be very confusing and deceptive for others. You have to be honest with yourself. If your intention is to get to the place where you believe you have let go but you are *still* not ready to forgive, then you have more work to do. You remain, to an extent, in the place of being right and you are getting a pay-off from being there, whatever that may be. You cannot rush this process, so keep digging deep to discover what's getting in the way of your freedom.

Forgiveness Is Never a Sign of Weakness

You will need a great deal of inner strength and personal understanding to forgive. You will have to feel sure that you no longer need your anger as armour to protect you from the hurt beneath. You no longer need to hold on to pain to hide from rebuilding your life.

What Does Forgiveness Cost?

The Hebrew word for forgiveness means two things: to remit a debt and to pay it. It's the same word for both. Forgiveness in the Christian New

Testament means literally 'to let go' and 'to cancel a debt'. To me, remitting and paying for a debt means taking responsibility for incurring the debt in the first place. By paying the debt you take back responsibility for all the choices you make in your life. Similarly, by letting go and cancelling the debt you are able to move directly into freedom. This applies to every situation in life. Forgiveness is the key to freedom.

What Forgiveness Is

Forgiveness is the beginning of your new life. Forgiveness happens in the present exactly where you are right now. It doesn't deny past hurts, it doesn't ignore the need for change or repentance for a past injury. It's about being willing to drop any barriers, to stop playing games and take the initiative towards restoring some kind of working relationship with your ex. It's about noticing for the first time how much energy you have wasted and how much damage you are doing to your own well-being by not forgiving.

Forgiveness Restores Your Self-esteem

By no longer identifying yourself with your past, you are able to do what I did when I said 'I am no longer willing to be a victim.' I said to myself 'I have been hurt enough in the past, I don't need to add to the hurt by punishing myself further.' It's about saying no to pain and yes to healing.

Forgiveness Is the End of the War

When you decide to end the war in your head and your body (because you cannot separate the two), you no longer have the desire to get even or make your ex suffer for what they have 'done' to you. As I said, sometimes justice just isn't meted out in the way you would enforce it if you made the rules – and you know, even if it were, it would not help your healing process. You just cannot undo what's been done, and your personal healing process has nothing to do with your ex. Ending the war within yourself means moving towards inner peace. It's about realizing that we are not forgiving them for *their* sake. We are forgiving for *our* sake and for our own peace of mind.

Forgiveness Is Positive Energy
Having wasted more than enough time in 'being right' or blaming 'them', forgiveness allows us to concentrate on rebuilding our own lives and creating a fabulous future. Ultimately forgiveness is a way of dealing honestly with the past and healing our inner pain. It will change your attitude to your life and will manifest itself through all the actions you take, and will allow you to heal your heart and love again.

Ultimate Release Exercises

The following two exercises will help you let go of anything that stands in the way of your achieving full recovery from your divorce and returning to a wellness that offers peace of mind, clarity and harmony. I suggest you do them in the order I have presented them for optimum effectiveness. Used diligently, they offer you amazing results.

The Ultimate Forgiveness Exercise
Imagine you are standing in front of your ex. You can see from the top of their head right down to their shoes. Stand a few feet away from them and look into their eyes. Out loud, say the following:

'I release you.'

'I let you go.'

'I cancel your debt and release your offence to me.'

'You owe me nothing.'

'I release my desire to get even with you.'

'I am complete.'

If you find this difficult, keep practising. It's not going to happen overnight for most people, though it might for some. Saying the words at first will sound unbelievable to you. That's OK – didn't it feel strange the first time you rode a bike or learned to swim? Practise. With practice, doing what's not natural right now will soon seep into your psyche and become something you don't even have to think about any more. Each day, see your ex standing in front of you (no, don't hide your eyes and squirm in your chair, you are past that now) and then speak out loud. Only by hearing the words come out of your mouth will you experience your forgiveness as a reality.

The Ultimate Goodbye Letter
The next way to say goodbye to your relationship is to commit it to paper. In this exercise you are asked to acknowledge both the good and the bad by taking it all out of your head and writing it down. This exercise is poignant in many ways, and everybody's goodbye letter is as unique as their individual relationship. Don't think about it, just blurt it all out. No one can tell you what to write, but here is a composite example which contains lines from

the hundreds of goodbye letters that my clients have written over the years.

- Goodbye to your dishonesty and secretiveness.
- Goodbye to having someone to come home to.
- Goodbye to your nagging and whinging.
- Goodbye to your terrible cooking.
- Goodbye to your emotional coldness.
- Goodbye to your delicious cheesecake.
- Goodbye to your lack of understanding.
- Goodbye to your lack of appreciation and support for me.
- Goodbye to your outrageous spending habits.
- Goodbye to your snoring caused by your chain-smoking.
- Goodbye to our dreams of the house in France.
- Goodbye to seeing our grandchildren grow up together.
- Goodbye to retiring to Brighton.
- Goodbye to your impatience and criticisms.

Once you have exhausted yourself (and this could take several days) you are invited to your own bonfire party.

Take your letter outside to a safe area. Put a match to it and let it burn. Ashes to ashes, dust to dust.

The Spiritual Divorce

Over the years I have noticed that there is something quite spiritual about truly letting go and forgiving. For me the process of letting go of my ex-husband is now on a 'soul level', which means that if I look deep inside, no matter what happened and how either of us behaved, I cannot find a single space inside me that holds any regret or bad feeling towards him. It's a spirit feeling. My spirit is free of pain, and of all its 'if onlys'.

Time is a great healer, although it's true to say that as I write this almost 14 years have passed since my divorce. However, I have felt this way for many years now, and as the years go by my feelings of compassion for him and freedom from him have led me to a deep level of learning about myself and an understanding of who I am in relationship. I would never have experienced this without the special gift that my ex was for me. That gift lives in my heart where I believe my spirit resides. Your spiritual divorce is about reaching that place inside yourself where your soul can breathe easily.

Spiritually divorcing is divorcing yourself from any energy that takes you away from your own free spirit. In order to begin the journey for yourself (and some people are already further along the way than they might think), there a few specific areas to acknowledge.

Your partner brought out many traits in you. Some good and some, well, let's just say they were more interesting than others. This was your ex's job and they did it incredibly well. These traits were lessons for you. Did you learn them?

Right now, write down every single trait and behaviour your ex brought out in you. For example, did they bring out:

- caring
- devotion
- sense of fun

- lethargy
- lack of self-esteem
- pride
- anger
- warmth
- humour
- disgust?

Check your list of traits. Each of them is a lesson in disguise. To move into a place that is more in touch with your spirit of self-awareness, ask yourself:

- What was the purpose of experiencing these traits?
- What did experiencing these traits teach me about what I don't want?
- What did they teach me about what I *do* want?
- How will experiencing them help me to move forward in my life?

Isn't it interesting that you have these insights? If you had not had your ex as your teacher, you would have missed out on a personal wisdom that will stand you in good stead as you design your new life in a different way.

Drop the Drama

Are you a person who attracts all kinds of controversy? Do you always have stories to tell that begin with 'It could only happen to me'? When you hear about how terrible someone else's divorce is, do you often think, 'Yeah, that's terrible, but you won't believe what *my* ex did'? If this sounds like you, then you are still in the drama of your divorce. So what are you resisting? Think about it. If you were to drop the drama, who would you be? Take your time to mull it over. There's no rush. But know that whilst you still hold on to the drama you will not be free.

Rewrite Your Script

Letting your soul take the reins of your life means you can rewrite the script for your life according to your true values. Previously, when you didn't know how to do it differently, you were in reaction to your life. Stuff happened and you connected it to similar stuff that had happened in your past. Rewriting your script gives you the opportunity to choose your life from a much deeper knowing of yourself. When you speak from a place of your spirit, you are honouring your own values and rules for your life. This takes an immense amount of courage, and a degree of risk. You could be rejected because your honesty may mean that the people currently in your life are challenged by you. Some of these people may find the 'new' you difficult to adjust to, and it would be easy for you to fall back into conforming or complying. However, is that what you want? It's your choice.

Spiritual Freedom

'Set your spirit free, it's the only way to be' – **The Spice Girls**

Above my desk I have a picture of myself, aged three, sitting in a very pretty dress with a big bow round it. My chubby little legs are dangling off the edge of the settee in my T-bar shoes, and I have a cheeky little grin on my face. I look at this photo daily because that little girl reminds me that I just want to get down and play. Right now as I write this, my urge is to go outside and have fun with the other 'children'. These days this can mean having afternoon tea at Kenwood House on Hampstead Heath and hearing the birds sing and seeing the flowers, breathing the air, allowing my body and mind to enjoy the freedom of relaxation away from my computer and the phone. It's also sitting on my favourite rock in a Mallorca hideaway hotel and watching the waves crash and the sun sparkle on the water. It's where I set my spirit free and, even as I write this, I can feel my spirit rise inside me. It's the same feeling I had when I was three years old. It's the only way to be.

Your spiritual divorce is about finding that freedom within yourself. It's about letting go of any feelings that suffocate your soul and exchanging them for a new attitude which, at least a few times every day, focuses on finding the pleasure in your life.

Your spirit is joyous, if you would only let it come out to play. This is not a religious experience – though sometimes it can be that, too, for some people. But whatever you believe in that dwells outside yourself, this is about freeing your inner self, your soul, and being present every day to experiencing and appreciating daily pleasure. Is it raining? Then go to the window and notice how the rain bounces off the ground, how it falls on the branches of the trees. Be present and free your spirit. Don't take anything for granted. We settle for far too little pleasure during our everyday lives. Many people are waiting for the weekend or their annual holiday to let go and feel joy. The truth is you can let go and experience being in spirit whenever you want. If you want to practise this, just get yourself a large elastic band and wear it on your wrist. Several times during the day, just snap it to wake yourself up. Look around you or out of the window and focus on something – anything will do. Really see it. Stay present with it for a moment, let any other thoughts go as you let yourself experience it. You are setting your spirit free and surrendering to the feeling of being alive.

When you make this a daily practice you begin to realize how much time most of us spend on automatic pilot and how little time we spend in spirit. In the moment that you focus on something else and stay present you are no longer in pain about anything. It hasn't gone away, so what happened? You got reconnected to you, that's what happened.

Reasons to be Grateful

It would be challenging to believe you had spiritually divorced unless you were able to be 'grateful' to your ex-partner for all that he or she taught you. In order for you to move towards a future relationship with your ex-partner, especially if there are children involved, being grateful is the final act of letting go. The last exercise I offer you here is about gratitude. It's about saying thank you to your ex-partner for everything you can remember, from the acceptable right through to the wonderful. Before you put your fingers down your own throat, give it a go. I have not steered you badly up to now, so trust me, I'm the Divorce Doctor!

The Ultimate Thank-you Letter

The ultimate thank-you letter is about holding your partner in your mind as your greatest gift, your ultimate teacher and someone you once cared enough about to marry/live with/start a family with. So let me start you off:

Dear Hannah

Thank you for our first date when you were so full of fun and made

---

me laugh. Thank you for taking care of me when I had to go into hospital after cutting my finger with the electric carving knife on Christmas Day. Thank you for our two beautiful children and for being a wonderful mother. Thank you for introducing me to Steve, who gave me my first order when I started the business. Thank you for making me laugh when you told me about your trip to India. Thank you for teaching me what I want from a relationship and how to behave so that I can get that next time. Thank you for being so kind to my father before he died ...

Your Thank-You Letter

Take yourself somewhere that sets your spirit free in your mind. Spend some time visiting your special place and let the good feelings rise inside you. This is a peaceful place for you, somewhere if you breathe deeply and let the outside sounds disappear, you will be able to hear the voice of your soul. Listen very carefully and let that inner place write this letter. Notice that what you write is the truth and cannot be denied. When you are finished, read it back to yourself out loud. Think about what your life from now on would be like if you held on to an attitude of gratitude to your ex. How would you feel inside yourself on a daily basis? How would you talk about your ex to other people from this place? How would you communicate with your ex from an attitude of gratitude? How would this attitude benefit your children?

Reasons to be Grateful Journal

Your Divorce Diary is now complete. Close the book and put it away somewhere out of sight. I'd rather you didn't look at it for at least two years. By that time you will be very different and it will be an interesting experience to look back over this period of your life with the benefit of hindsight.

You are into recovery and you have survived. So now it's time to create your 'Reasons to be Grateful Journal'. I have one of these by my bedside, and at least three times a week before I go to sleep I make an entry. I can usually think of at least six reasons to be grateful for something that happened during the day or for something or someone I already have in my life. It's a wonderful thing to do because it sets my spirit free before I go to sleep, and usually leads to lovely dreams. Sometimes I think of challenges during the day. I first started this journal many years ago when my children were young and I remember trying hard not to get mad when arriving to pick my kids up from school if 'that woman' had got my space, and then being so grateful that I wasn't parked there when a rogue lawnmower rolled into her passenger door. I remember trying not to fuss over an upturned bowl of cereal on my clean floor when my young son chirpily said, 'There's no point crying over spilt milk, Mummy' and made me laugh. Nowadays I write about how grateful I am that I go on holidays with my daughter and spend quality time with my son, have amazing clients to work with and friends and family I love, trust and support just as they love, trust and support me. I urge you to keep a journal like this and let the good times roll.

No Regrets

> *'Non, je ne regrette rien'.* - **Edith Piaf**

Regret is such a wasted emotion. Edith Piaf made the concept of 'no regrets' one that most of us are aware of through her famous song. I would love this to be your Swan Song for your marriage. No regrets. Game over. No more snakes and ladders, no more two paces forward and three back down again. It's time to move from conflict to co-operation. In this final exercise, especially if you have children, I'd like you to write an 'Agreement of Co-operation' with your ex that is as fair towards you both. Use everything you have learned in this chapter to write it. You may choose never to share it with your ex or even discuss it with them, or you may decide that you'd like your ex to create an agreement of their own and then invite them to sit down with you to negotiate an agreement that works for both of you. Creating this agreement is your intention for your relationship as you move forward.

If you don't have kids and your lives are not intertwined in any way, you may be able to say 'Goodbye, good luck and thank you for having me.' However, if you will continue to be connected for some time to come, what is your intention from today onwards? Will you be able to honour your values, communicate like an adult, stay in spirit and let go without regret? It's a tall order, I know, but I also know that you are perfectly capable of pulling it off. If you want to.

Personal Prescription for Your Full Recovery: Five-day Treatment

Directions for Use

This is your last prescription. Your full recovery is imminent and it's based on letting go of conflict and moving towards co-operation. It's time to learn how to dance on a shifting floor and embrace – rather than resist – the changes life is offering you.

Your Reasons to Be Grateful Journal is now a vital tool in keeping you present in your life and appreciating everything that will keep you buoyant in your life.

Dosage

Every day for the next year you are required to write in your Reasons to Be Gratitude Journal. Write down six things that you are grateful for each day, from your healthy body to remembering your umbrella on a rainy day. Keep this journal for a full year before you review it.

Self-affirmation Medicine

- Today is a good day. Today I will say 'I can handle it' to everything that happens.
- Today I will let go of anything that holds me back. I am moving forward with my wonderful life.
- I am proud of my strengths and my courage. I have everything I need to succeed.
- I choose to make the best of what I have, every day of my life.
- I will trust myself and respect the process of my changing life and all that it is teaching me.
- I am free to create the life I choose in every moment.
- I am a survivor and I love that about myself.

Chapter 10
Wellness – the New You!

Awareness	Of what you really want
Attitude	How you express your needs and desires
Action	What you are willing to do to embrace the New You!

*'Your work is to discover your world; and, then,
with all your heart, give yourself to it.'* - **Buddha**

Clever chap, Buddha – he certainly knew his stuff. For someone who never got married or divorced, he understood the true essence of being human. Using his wise words as a model for your future, this chapter really is about embracing your wellness, discovering your rules for your life and living them fully each and every day.

You have come such a long way and now, finally, it's done. The papers have been signed, you've settled your finances, you have sorted out where you will both be living and the kids know when they will see their other parent. You are feeling better than you have for a very long time. You are stepping into a time of personal growth, re-evaluating your life and taking back control. Freedom and your new identity beckon.

In this chapter you are going to create a set of operating instructions for your new life. These will come from your personal values; when you know your values in every area of your life you can make choices for the future that are in alignment with who you are and what you want to be, do and have.

We have already created your values for your career, so you have an idea of how it works. It's time to take this one step further. Of all the work that I do with my clients, I believe that this is the most personal and the most important. Without understanding or becoming familiar with your values in every area of your life, it's very easy to end up living life according to someone else's values. There are a lot of people out there who know exactly what they want. If you are not sure about what *you* want, you'll end up living life their way, not yours.

You are stepping out into the world as a single person. This is a whole new ball game. There are some new boundaries you'll need to put into place in order to protect yourself and stay true to who you are and what you want. It's very easy in the early stages to say 'yes' to all kinds of requests pertaining to work, family requirements and social arrangements. Unless you have some personal guidelines to live by, you may find yourself overstretched and overwhelmed. As I said previously, every time you say 'yes' to something, you are saying 'no' to something else. You cannot put boundaries into place and know what to agree to and what to decline unless you understand the impact your decisions will have on your personal values.

Living life according to your values is a radical act. However, unless you have any wish to repeat mistakes from the past, radical is now where it's at for you.

If Your Soul Could Speak

I often say that if your soul could speak, it would articulate itself through your values. When you speak to people who are depressed you will discover that they are not living in alignment with their personal values because most of them have never really figured out what those are in the first place. By the time they get to the depressed stage, so many of their values have been violated, either by themselves or by others, that they are firmly stuck or frozen in a state of numbness. Try telling a depressed person that it will all be OK and that they should try to pull themselves together and they will look at you as if you are crazier than they feel. They are so 'pressed down' that their identity has been crushed and it's not an easy job to rebuild it.

Being well and maintaining wellness mean that you understand your own needs and surround yourself with people and situations that honour your being who you really are.

Right now we are going to begin rebuilding your identity. Let's start with creating your own personal blueprint for a successful life ahead.

Your Rules, Your Life

I have found that most people can divide their lives into around eight basic categories:

1. Health and wellbeing
2. Family and friends
3. Intimate relationships
4. Career
5. Money
6. Environment – where you live and work
7. Fun and recreation
8. Personal growth/spiritual development/religion

We have already looked at career, and I want you to put intimate relationship on hold till later in this chapter, but we can address each

of the other areas of your life and use the same template that we used
before to write your own rules for each area.

Values = 'Must Haves'	Definitions
	What would Ideal [name of value] provide me with?
	What would have to happen in order for me to experience Ideal [name of value]?
	What am I willing to do to achieve Ideal [name of value] and when will I begin?
	What would happen if I didn't have Ideal [name of value]?
Name of value (for example 'Ideal Good Health and Wellbeing'	What would Ideal Good Health and Wellbeing provide me with?: Vitality, energy, lightness, happiness, security What would have to happen in order for me to experience Ideal Good Health and Wellbeing?: I'd have to believe I deserved to have it/I'd have to eat less and exercise more/I'd have to believe it was possible to lose weight by sticking to a plan What do Ideal Good Health and Wellbeing provide others with?: They would be able to have more fun with me/I could go hill-walking/I would feel great undressed/I could breathe more easily What am I willing to do to achieve Ideal Good Health and Wellbeing?: I'm not willing to do anything right now What would happen if I didn't experience Ideal Good Health and Wellbeing?: I'd carry on moaning about my body/I may not live long enough to see my grandchildren/I won't have the confidence to find a new mate/my lungs will give up/and nothing would change.

Fill in a new template for each value. Take your time to complete your answers to each question. Ask yourself over and over, 'What will that provide me with …?' until there is nothing more to add.

Over the next few days, go back to tweak and add until you have created your rules for every area of your life.

Using Your Rules as a Guide

Once you have a complete blueprint of your personal values, the next thing is to check out how satisfied you are that you are honouring them in your life.

Scoring Your Values

Take 'health and wellbeing' and look down your list of criteria for this value. Right now, on a scale from 1 to 10 (10 being 'Yes, I am satisfied that I have all this in my life' and 1 being 'I don't have any of this in my life'), what's your score? Usually the first score you think of is the right score for you. If you scored 7 or below, the gap between what you want and what you are getting is too big right now. You are not living according to the rules for your own life. You know what you want and yet you are not getting it, so what stands in your way?

Let me give you an example. Perhaps you enjoy going out to eat in nice restaurants. I call you and tell you that a new restaurant has opened up near you. I say that the food is OK, a bit hit and miss; some of the tables have tablecloths and some don't and the waiters are nice but some are a bit smelly. And then I say to you, 'Would you like to go for your birthday?' Should I be surprised to hear that you are less than enthusiastic? The reason is that you have higher standards than that. You don't want to eat in a mediocre restaurant, you don't want to watch a mediocre film just because it's somewhere to eat your popcorn, and you don't want mediocre friends or a mediocre job. So why would you settle for mediocre health and wellbeing?

It's now time to set yourself standards. No one can do this for you, it's your job. No one else knows what your personal values are better than you. In order for you to be fully self-expressed in your life and speak from a place of your personal values, you had better be very clear about what they are.

Expressing Yourself from Your Values

Annie had been divorced for a year when she came to see me because she was having a problem expressing herself without getting angry or bursting into tears. This is exactly how she had behaved in her marriage, always scared to say what she wanted and then waiting until she was so exasperated that it came out the wrong way. She had moved on and was happily socializing with her friends and getting used to being single, but one girlfriend, Tina, pressed her buttons. Tina was continuously late whenever they went out. It didn't matter if it was popping out for coffee, meeting up for a meal or going dancing. In the past Annie would have followed her old pattern and said it was OK because she didn't want to upset people, then later feel resentment. She was tempted to do this because Tina's friendship was more important to her than ever now that she was single. However, she felt the familiar resentful feelings bubbling up and realized that she was snapping at Tina for things that were completely irrelevant. In order to get past this once and for all, she simply had to tell Tina how she felt. When we created Annie's values she discovered that 'ideal friendships' would provide her with friends who were reliable, kept their word and, give or take ten minutes, arrived on time. Clearly Tina trod all over this value for Annie. As I mentioned back in Chapter 7, I learned a long time ago from one of my great teachers, Anthony Robbins, that 'It's never the person, the situation or the circumstance that will ever upset or frustrate me; it's always the value of mine that has been dishonoured or violated.'

I explained to Annie that it wasn't Tina who was upsetting her. In fact, it could never be a person or a situation or a circumstance; it was Annie's personal value that she was not able to honour with Tina and which Tina continuously violated. Knowing this is very good news indeed. It means that instead of blaming Tina, Annie can speak from a place of her values and let Tina know how Tina's behaviour affects her.

Do you remember the four-part messages? Well, they now take on a whole new meaning when used to express your values.

> Annie's message to Tina looked something like this:
> When you arrived late for our meal tonight and for coffee last week and for dancing on Friday [specific behaviour], I felt hurt [my emotion] because I cannot rely on you and I am left waiting for you, which is uncomfortable for me and wastes my own time [the impact on me]. What I want is for you to keep your word and turn up on time so that I know our friendship is as important to you as it is to me [my desired outcome].

Expressing yourself from your values allows the other person to know exactly how their behaviour has affected you. This way you are not playing the blame game by saying, 'Why can't you be on time for once?' or being aggressive. At the same time, you need to understand that even though, for example, 'being on time' is important to you, the other person may not have a value around this. Perhaps they are far more laid back and would not have any anxiety if you were late. When you understand your own values you begin to realize that other people have their own, very different, ones.

> In fact, in Tina's case this was true. She didn't wear her watch outside work and was relaxed about her free time. When she realized how her behaviour affected Annie, she agreed to do her utmost to be on time.

Sometimes you may need to negotiate and come to a mutual compromise that honours both your values. But this type of co-operation makes it much easier to hold on to your own boundaries in future relationships.

What Do You Really Want?

Your values can be used in yet another way. Often clients tell me that they feel a bit lost after divorce. This is understandable. Once part of a unit, they are now single; and whilst they know they are free to design their life their way, they are not sure what 'their way' is.

To find your way back to you, just check out your values. Your career value has already given you a new purpose for your life and shown you what needs to happen in order for you to fulfil that purpose. In turn, your values in each of the other areas of your life will give you back your identity.

> Your values are the specific ingredients of your identity.

When you are true to yourself, you begin to attract the people and situations that naturally lead you in the right direction. You can trust that life will unfold exactly as it should and present the right opportunities for your growth. When you follow your own guidelines for living, you will be in the right place at the right time with exactly the right people around you. Don't take my word for it. Try it out. Your personal prescription at the end of this chapter will explain exactly what you need to do.

I cannot guarantee you specific outcomes – in fact, that's the fun of it. The trick is to live in alignment with your values without being attached to any specific outcomes. You always have the desire and the intention of achieving what you want – in fact, I'd like you to be very clear about what you want – but stay open to receiving your desires in some unpredictable ways. If the paths that open up before you can be travelled whilst keeping to your values, then travel them. If they cannot, don't take them.

Your heart and soul speak to you through your values. Explaining this reminds me of a wonderful poem from Carlos Castaneda's 'The Teachings of Don Juan', which encapsulates exactly what I wish for you.

> *Anything is one of a million paths. Therefore you must*
> *always keep in mind that a path is only a path; if you*
> *feel you should not follow it, you must not stay with it*
> *under any conditions. To have such clarity you must lead a*
> *disciplined life. Only then will you know that any path is*
> *only a path and there is no affront, to oneself or to others,*
> *in dropping it if that is what your heart tells you to do. But*
> *your decision to keep on the path or to leave it must*
> *be free of fear or ambition. I warn you. Look at every*
> *path closely and deliberately. Try it as many times as*
> *you think necessary. Then ask yourself:*
> *… Does this path have a heart? If it does, the path is good;*
> *if it doesn't, it is of no use. Both paths lead nowhere; but*
> *one has a heart, the other doesn't. One makes for a joyful*
> *journey; as long as you follow it, you are one with it.*
> *The other will make you curse your life. One makes you*
> *strong; the other weakens you.*
> *… The trouble is nobody asks the question; and when a man*
> *finally realizes that he has taken a path without a heart,*

the path is ready to kill him. At that point very few men
can stop to deliberate, and leave the path. A path without a
heart is never enjoyable. You have to work hard even to take
it. On the other hand, a path with heart is easy; it does not
make you work at liking it.
… For me there is only the travelling on the paths that
have a heart, on any path that may have a heart.
There I travel, and the only worthwhile challenge for
me is to traverse its full length. And there I travel –
looking, looking, breathlessly.

Being Single Again

Your new path is such an exciting one to travel, and I promise that your heart will definitely open up along the way. Right now you are a free agent and it's important that you bring some light-hearted activities into your life and make some necessary deposits in your 'fun bank'.

If you are like most people I meet, you will, at some point, be ready to dip your toe back into dating. Whilst that may seem like a scary proposition right now, most people would like to think of themselves enjoying a wonderful future with someone they love and who loves them. Although that may be a little way down the path right now, the first step is feeling comfortable with yourself again.

Enjoying You

Learn to enjoy your own company. Being by yourself, choosing what you want to eat, watching what you want on TV and running life according to your own schedule can be very satisfying indeed. In fact, it is absolutely necessary that you learn how to make yourself happy in your own company, otherwise you may find yourself spending time with people who are not right for you just to avoid being alone.

Can I Be Alone?

I want you to make a clear distinction here. *Being alone is different from being lonely.* I can remember lying on a hammock on a gorgeous beach during the last holiday of my marriage and realizing that I had never felt lonelier in my entire life. I felt numb and disconnected. Now I am grateful for that experience, because it created the distinction for me between being lonely and being alone.

Being comfortable being alone happens when you are at peace within yourself.

Looking After You

You begin to be comfortable with being alone by being willing to take care of yourself without using food, the TV, alcohol or anything else to hide from the world. The following questions will give you an idea about how comfortable you are with being independent:

* Do I fill up my days and nights with busy-ness?
* What would I do if I made time for me?
* What kind of people would I choose to be with?

Your answers will allow you to raise your awareness about how comfortable you are with your new situation. If you believe you can be happy being single, then single will become an acceptable lifestyle for you. Instead of begrudging time spent with family and friends because you think you should be 'out there' finding a new partner, you'll have a renewed appreciation for the people in your life who care for you – and that will bring you a very special kind of contentment and peace.

If you have lived with another adult for more than 10, 20 or even 30 years, being on your own can feel very strange at first. Some people will feel so liberated that they are buoyed along by a surge of energy and a sense of freedom at first. However, when the first bout of euphoria settles down, everyone who has been in a long-term relationship has to come to terms with a different way of life. When you are able to feel comfortable on your own, you will know for sure that you are healing well and regaining your identity.

When Annabel left Liam after 12 years of marriage, Liam was completely lost. He did not know how to be on his own. He couldn't even watch an hour's TV alone, so he spent every waking hour at work, and if he wasn't meeting friends or clients in the evening for drinks or dinner he was on his mobile phone until he went to sleep. After six months of this he was absolutely exhausted.

I suggested he begin with one evening a week at home on his own. He said that he would try it and that the best night was Monday as he had been out all weekend, but it was vital he had a plan for the evening from the moment he walked through the door. He decided the first thing he would do was take off his suit and have a shower. He would put on something very comfortable and then he would pour one glass of wine or have a beer and prepare his meal. He was a great cook and loved Thai food. So he decided he would cook a different Thai meal each week. This meant he had to make sure he had the ingredients he needed, which he agreed he would buy at the weekend. Liam also loved jazz and was always buying CDs that he never had a chance to listen to properly. So the music would accompany his preparations. He would then eat his meal whilst reading the paper. He had a great coffee machine and he would have coffee after his meal by the TV. He didn't enjoy TV that much, so he was concerned with what he would do with the rest of the evening if he didn't get back on the phone. I asked him what he had enjoyed as a boy. It turned out he was great at huge complicated jigsaws and making model cars.

So he bought a 5,000-piece jigsaw and a classic car model and began the process.

On the Tuesday after his first Monday night, Liam called me. Everything had been running according to plan until he'd sat down with his meal. He told me that he had begun to cry and that he could not even swallow his food. He had cried for quite a while and gone to bed. He said that this 'being alone stuff' was very hard and he didn't think it was a good idea. I asked Liam what he thought the tears were for and he said it felt like he was spending time with a stranger and he realized he really didn't know himself very well. He didn't know how to 'be' with himself and it had frightened and shocked him. He realized that it wasn't Annabel that he missed; it was simply the presence of another person. He said that he felt like he was frightened of himself because he didn't know how to be his own friend. I completely understood how he felt.

However, the following Monday he tried again. This time he got as far as coffee, cried again but decided to do an area of the huge jigsaw. He had become absorbed, and with his new CD playing in the background, he was aware of his heavy heart but spent a good couple of hours feeling more peaceful. By the third Monday he was looking forward to his time alone, especially as he wanted to try out a new recipe which he would be using to cook for friends that Friday.

Liam now has two designated nights a week to himself and treasures them.

It takes practice to see your time alone as a very special treat. For those of us who have families to manage, time alone will be much rarer. Even more reason to cherish it and enjoy the pleasure of making yourself happy. You can become your own best friend. No one will ever be able to treat you as well as you can treat yourself, because you know you better than anyone else. This is not something to be afraid of – even though, at first, like Liam, you may feel you don't know yourself well enough to give yourself a treat. Even if the only time you get is in the bath, get the very best bath oil you can afford, light some scented candles, waterproof your iPod and sink into bliss for at least 20 minutes. With practice, you can learn to take pleasure in being alone.

Have Some Fun

It's vital to have some fun now you are single. Find something that you have always wanted to do. One client of mine took up juggling, another learned salsa dancing, and another lady, who had not laughed for a very long time, took herself off to the Edinburgh Festival and spent a week going from one comedy gig to another, met some great people and had the most fun she had had in years.

If you cannot bear the thought of taking up a new hobby or travelling alone (which I would highly recommend because it really is a liberating experience), see if you can get a friend to go along with you.

Making new friends is important when you are newly single, and whilst it takes courage to go on singles holidays, join groups and get out there on your own, the comfort is that everyone else at these groups feels pretty much the same as you. Once you make the effort to show up, you'll find people friendly and welcoming.

Remember, this is your life and you are entitled to be happy. Laughter is the very best medicine of all. When you can laugh out loud in the face of all you have been through, your wellbeing will soar.

Personal Freedom

As you move into a place of personal freedom it's time to work on any old issues that remain. Perhaps there are some old upsets or beliefs that you need to let go of. Perhaps some unresolved relationships with people in your past and even your present that stand in the way of complete wellness. Now is the time to address any loose ends that need tying up.

Look at taking on a coach who will get you into action. Spend more time understanding your own values, or maybe you'd like to dig even deeper and see a counsellor to explore feelings that are still bothering you. Invest time now in your own personal development. Take some courses, read some books and be open to exercises like yoga, tai chi and dance, like the wonderful Nia which combines the strength of martial arts with the wisdom of healing forms of body work. Call me if you'd like my support. Do anything that engages your body and soul. In this way you can supercharge your healing.

Owning Your Identity

All of the above is designed to get you back in touch with your own identity so that you can feel it in your bones rather than intellectually in a rational way. It's like taking off any clothes that don't fit and replacing them with a made-to-measure 'identity suit'. From this place you can drop any masks and be yourself. You can face the world and be more open with people, while always having your boundaries in place. Remember that your boundaries come from understanding what you can and cannot allow, and how people can and cannot behave in your company. Personal boundaries will gain you respect from others and personal respect for yourself. Use your values to show you where your boundaries are, so that you can be open and yet protected all at the same time.

Trusting Yourself

From this new place of being, you begin to trust yourself more and more. The more you are able to honour your values and keep your boundaries in place, the more evidence you will have that you can trust yourself in any circumstance.

Because you now know how to communicate to avoid giving mixed messages, you have evidence that you can be fully expressed in a way that is clear and understandable.

Because you are surrounding yourself with people who honour your values, it is much easier to discern those who cannot be trusted.

Because you know how to draw back if someone betrays that trust, you have evidence that you can protect yourself. By taking small risks with your feelings and observing the results, you will intuitively know when you are healed enough to contemplate a love relationship again. And when you can risk being yourself in relationship, without thinking you will fall to pieces if it ends, you know that it's time to consider being in a new relationship.

From First Date to Soulmate

Getting back out on the dating scene is a big deal. There is much to consider about how, who and when to date. The rest of this chapter looks at dating from first date to soulmate and all the stages in between. Because you have been in a long-term relationship, the process is different from when you were young, free and single with no baggage. You are not a starry-eyed teen. Time is more important to you now, and whilst you want to take it slowly you don't want to waste your time.

Creating Designer Relationships

Did you know that you can design your next relationship however you want it to be? In seminars that I run I show people how to design a relationship that fits exactly with their values and their lifestyle.

After my own divorce I was very clear that I wanted to be in a monogamous relationship but did not want to live with anyone. I was exceptionally clear about the kind of man I wanted to be with. He had to be someone who had children of his own whom he adored as much as I adored my own. He would have to understand that I wanted to raise my kids without becoming the 'Brady Bunch', so it had to be someone who would not need to live with me.

Frogs and Frogesses and Princes and Princesses

I have found that the clearer your idea of what you want (and that applies to anything you want in your life), the more likely you are to receive it. After sifting through several 'frogs', I finally found my prince. Before that there was a point when I was almost tempted to cast aside my rules, but when I checked this person against my Ideal Intimate Relationship value he fell short, so I kept up the search until I found exactly the right man.

I want you to be able to design your perfect relationship because I believe that it's not until you are clear about what you want that it can come your way. Many of the fabulous personal development experts such as Wayne Dyer, Esther and Jerry Hicks, Deepak Chopra and Lynn Grabhorn, to name a few of my personal favourites, all agree that knowing what you want, aligning it with your values and believing that you deserve it will conspire with the universe to have it sent to you. I have evidence of this because it's exactly what happened to me and to every one of my clients who followed these guidelines.

Your Perfect Partner

So now I think you are ready to go out 'shopping' for your next partner. Like any good shopper, it helps to have a detailed list so that you don't forget anything. Sometimes we are seduced by perfect packaging rather than what's inside. We can be easily tempted, but don't be fooled. It takes a while to get to know someone. No one reveals everything in the early days of dating. You need to 'interview' subtly and discreetly for the job of being your perfect partner.

The Perfect Partner Template

You've probably guessed that it's your values that will help you to create your shopping list for your new mate. Using the template below I would like you to create your Ideal Intimate Relationship value. I have inserted some examples to give you some ideas. Once again, take your time and do this thoroughly. Keep checking back and tweak it until it reads perfectly for you.

Values = 'Must Haves'	Definitions
	What would an Ideal Intimate Relationship provide me with? What would have to happen in order for me to experience an Ideal Intimate Relationship? What am I willing to do to achieve an Ideal Intimate Relationship? What would happen if I didn't have an Ideal Intimate Relationship?
Ideal Intimate Relationship	What would an Ideal Intimate Relationship provide me with?: Fun, someone to have adventures with, someone to talk to and share my interests with, someone to learn from, someone who showed me care and attention and who listened to me. Someone who keeps their word/whom I can trust, etc. What would have to happen in order for me to experience an Ideal Intimate Relationship?: I'd need to find someone who honours my values, I'd have to be willing to take a risk that I might get hurt again, I'd need to know I could trust myself and leave if it wasn't working, etc.

	What am I willing to do to achieve an Ideal Intimate Relationship?: I am willing to go out on dates from January. I am willing to be all the values I want to see in my new relationship. I am willing to take responsibility for creating a growing relationship, etc. What would happen if I didn't experience an Ideal Intimate Relationship?: I would know that I was not ready yet, or I would have made the decision not to be in a relationship. I would know that I was sticking to my rules for relationships and I would need to review them if I truly wanted a loving relationship.

Once you have created your list of criteria for your ideal relationship you have your 'relationship shopping list'.

What You Cannot Live Without

There may be specific criteria on your list that are more important than others. There are no perfect people out there, but there are some specific values that you may not be able to live without. Perhaps honesty or open communication or fun? Look at your list and decide which are your top five 'must haves'. The rest would be a bonus and there is no reason to think that you won't find these qualities in your mate; however, the top five are non-negotiable and have to be there.

Your job is to find yourself some evidence that your mate can come up with the goods. If honesty, communication and fun are important to you, find evidence of honesty in their conversation, notice whether you are really having fun, hear how easily they communicate. When you get home from your date, take a moment to complete the Relationship Evaluator (overleaf). You are also looking for other values that they share with you.

Relationship Evaluator

Name: ....

       Physical Description: ....

       Personality: ....

       Quality of Conversation: ....

       Shared Values: ....

       Overall Score: ....

If less than 8 – what's the obstacle? ....

....

....

....

Score strength of obstacle (1–10): ....

Comments: ....

....

....

....

Decision: ....

Perhaps having a passion or interest other than work is important to you in a partner, perhaps you enjoy art, theatre, sport or the outdoors. Ask questions that help you discover what they enjoy doing with their free time. During early meetings, do *not* talk about ex-partners or spill your separation story. In the beginning keep conversation light and friendly. Have fun! When you get to know each other better, there will be plenty of time to talk in more depth.

Don't Give Up

Any time you find yourself dating someone who doesn't quite fit your criteria, just remind yourself that it isn't that easy to get the right 'fit'. How many times have you been out to buy a jacket or a pair of shoes and come back empty-handed? But you don't give up just because you couldn't find what you wanted. You keep shopping until you find it. Same with relationships. Have patience, keep to your list and you will find what you want in the end.

First Dates

Before we look at the different types of relationships that you may find yourself in, a word or two (or three) about first dates. There are some rules that apply and it's worth knowing what they are.

Meet in a Safe Place

I may be stating the blindingly obvious, but I don't care. Whatever you do, please meet somewhere safe. Let a friend or family member know where you are going and have your mobile with you. Safety is the first rule of dating. Even if you have been introduced by friends, don't share a car. It's far better to have your own transport or take a taxi. That way you are free to leave whenever you wish, you will avoid any awkwardness and are not in an enclosed space with someone you don't know. Enough said.

Dating Rules for Women

- Look great. Take time to make yourself look gorgeous for your date. You'll feel more confident and he will know you have made an effort, which will make you even more appealing.
- Don't give away too much. Stay a little enigmatic without being closed. Men love mystery; it keeps them interested in coming back for more.
- Get into shape. Sorry, but men are visual creatures. If they like what they see they will ask for another date. We are not talking about being thin. Men love well-proportioned women regardless of their size. It's about shape. A shapely silhouette is sexy. And most women will tell you that the happier they are with their body, the more confident they are.
- Let him pay. At least on the first couple of dates. It's his job to make sure you are fed and watered or bought popcorn. It gives him the opportunity to feel good about giving you a great time. Don't take it away from him.
- Always say 'thank you.' Men adore being appreciated, and saying 'thank you' lets them know that their effort is not wasted. When you thank him for a restaurant meal, a man feels like he has spent all day in the kitchen cooking it himself. Your appreciation wins you lots of brownie points.
- Don't be too available. Let him leave messages on your phone and don't ring back the same day if you can help it. By not appearing

desperate, he knows you are self-assured and confident and not waiting to marry him.

- Don't talk about your ex. Your date may hear something he can relate to himself that you didn't like about your ex and may feel hurt or embarrassed. Until you know someone very, very well, keep your counsel.

- Don't allow him to become possessive. If he shows signs of being clingy or needy, don't date him again. You may find that he wants a replacement wife, mother or someone he can control. Early signs are wanting to see you the next day, texting and phoning 24/7 and generally taking up far too much of your time. Is this what you need right now?

- Be interesting. Tell him about holidays you have been on, types of music you enjoy. Find out what he enjoys and keep the conversation light and positive.

- Come home and use your Relationship Evaluator to tick off his good points and decide whether you'd like to see him again. If you are unsure, keep dating him until you can be sure he's not for you. You will probably know this by the third or fourth date.

Dating Rules for Men

- Look your best. Smell good and dress smartly and cleanly. Women are put off by men who do not take care of their appearance.

- Don't be late. If you are meeting for a drink, get there earlier, arrange where you will sit and be prepared when your date arrives. Women love feeling taken care of and they love a man who cares enough to plan.

- Be interested. Stop talking and start listening. Women like to talk about themselves but will not do so if you spend the whole evening telling her about you. She will listen attentively but wonder if you are interested in her or just the sound of your own voice. One of the greatest compliments you can give her is to show interest in her and join in when appropriate.
- Compliment your date. Always tell your date how lovely she looks. She will have made a great deal of effort for you and it's wonderful for her to hear that you have noticed, so she will feel beautiful.
- Remember to have fun. Make her laugh and keep it light. Women love men who are entertaining and fun to be with.
- Don't drink too much. No woman wants to talk to a man whose eyes are glazed over. It's actually rude. Good manners and courtesy will get you points. Women love well-mannered men. The age of chivalry is *not* over.
- Be confident. Women love men who show that they are confident in their own skins. It allows them to trust in you and your ability to please her and take care of her.
- Be yourself. There is no point trying to be something you are not. You won't be able to keep it going and you will get found out. It's better to be who you are right from the beginning; if a woman likes you she will like you for who you are, not who you are pretending to be.
- The same rule applies here for men as it does for women. Come home and use your Relationship Evaluator to tick off her good points and decide whether you'd like to see her again. If you are unsure, keep dating her until you decide she's not for you. You will probably know this by the third or fourth date.

When's the Right Time for Sex?

Well, certainly not on the first date – even if you have been a nun or a monk for a year or more! Most men will not refuse if a women gives out certain signals, but from what I have heard, from so many men, it's still the case that many men have little respect for women who give it all away too soon. Someone I knew had sex on the first date because she said she was a 'grown up' and 'playing games' was not her style. Maybe she's right, but I've yet to meet a man who is that anxious for a second, third and fourth date – and neither has she. So here are some guidelines:

1st date   peck on cheek – at least one week before next date
2nd date   peck on cheek – at least one week before next date
3rd date   kiss on lips (not too long) – five days before next date
4th date   more kissing on lips (a bit longer) – five days before next date
5th date   more full-on kissing – at least four days before next date
6th date   more intimacy without full sex
7th date   it's up to you!

Some men and women maintain that this is still too fast, while others will ask what century I'm living in. In the end, only you can decide. But I would suggest you give yourself time to get to know someone and build up the desire. Once you have had sex you have crossed a line and you begin to move towards intimacy. Keep the suspense and excitement alive for you both. You may have the rest of your lives ahead. What's the rush?

Defibrillator Relationships: Restarting Your Heart

I often refer to the first relationship after divorce as a 'defibrillator' relationship: a relationship that restarts your heart. These are transitional relationships with someone you feel desirable and attractive around. Sometimes these relationships look like the answer to your prayers, and sometimes they are history repeating itself. Sometimes they last for a few months or a few years, and inevitably they will always raise some unresolved issues that you are carrying over from the past. That's the whole point of stepping-stone relationships. They are designed for trying out your new skills and strategies and for you to observe yourself as you come up against similar attitudes and behaviours that you experienced with your ex and perhaps in previous relationships.

It may occur to you that once again you have attracted a similar mate even though they don't seem to resemble your ex at all. You ask yourself, are all men like this? Do all women behave like that? It slowly dawns on you that the common denominator is you. Other people you know find different types of mates, but for some reason you seem to draw the same people to you over and over again. This time, use the opportunity to get to know yourself better. Understand that wherever you go and whomever you are with, you always take you with you. If you are attracted to the same kind of person over and over, there must be something you are doing to make this happen, you just haven't worked out what it is yet.

Until you understand your old wiring, and are *choosing* your responses instead of reacting as you have always done – and until you can take stock of your values, put your boundaries firmly in place and know exactly what you want from your ideal intimate relationship – you will keeping meeting the same mate in different guises.

If this happens, take a step back and re-evaluate. Work out what is happening, why it's happening and what you intend to do about it. Or just get in touch with me so that I or one of my team can help you.

More About Sex

I've talked about sex during the early stages of dating, but we need to explore the subject in more detail. Sex is bound to be on the agenda at some point. Many newly divorced men and women say that their sex drive is higher than ever after divorce. This is because it may have been many months since they last had sex and also because they are looking for the emotional closeness that making love brings. I remember a relative saying to me after my divorce, 'My dear, are you behaving in a way you'd like your children to behave?' As they were five and eight it seemed a funny question at the time, but I knew what she meant.

You need to be very clear for yourself what feels right and what doesn't as far as sex is concerned. It's really important not to let your libido run wild and instead have some perspective about your own moral and emotional stance. Whether you are male or female it's your job to take responsibility for your sexuality.

Most women I have spoken to say that, for them, sex is an emotional issue. It's also true to say that many women have had great fun with a one-night stand which they knew was just a fling, as long as they felt safe. However, once they are in a dating relationship, making love adds an emotional dimension for most women.

Whilst it may be exceptionally tempting to have the closeness that sex affords early on, be very clear about what sex means to you – and what it means to the other person.

Men and women are equally responsible for what happens in a relationship. Each must be clear about their boundaries. We all know that a nice dinner doesn't equal sex, nor does a comforting hug need to lead to anything more than a hug in return. Until you feel really comfortable about having sex, don't. Talk as openly as you can about how you feel and what you would like in terms of comfort other than sex. Holding hands and kissing may work well at first, and you need to be able to ask each other what works and what doesn't.

Sex also brings up the issue of where and when. This may involve bringing someone home, and if you have kids this is something that cannot be undertaken lightly. Everybody has their own morals on this, but I would suggest that it's something to think about so you are prepared when the situation arises.

As far as protection goes, always use a condom. You may have been with your last partner for many years, and perhaps your new mate assures you that they have not had any other partners, but better safe than sorry. Don't take unnecessary risks. If the other person can't respect this, they are not the person for you.

'Growing' Relationships

Some people have several 'growing' relationships. Each in its own way is a stepping stone for the next; if this is your experience I can guarantee you will learn something from each of them. The trick is to know when to end them and not fall back into the fear of being on your own again or thinking that you'll never find another person like this. Some of these relationships were not built to last. It's possible that one or both of you are mirroring the other in terms of getting over past partners. Perhaps you are consciously trying out new ways of behaving and new ways of responding. The more honest you can both be about what the relationship is about for you, the better. Let the other person know where you stand. If you want to keep it light and get to know each slowly, be clear about your boundaries. Stay very much in the present, and for goodness sake don't start planning your future together! Take it one date at a time, focus on enjoying the time together and see where it goes.

Barry had been married to Sue for 24 years. He had not seen his divorce coming and his recovery had taken the best part of two years. Much of this time had been spent resisting the truth that Sue was not coming back; as a result he had experienced a great deal of pain which he endured with the help of his best friend, Prozac. Finally, he was ready to date again and was fixed up with a blind date by a close friend. Mandy was pretty, bubbly and emotionally stable and it was hard for Barry to find anything wrong with her at all. But he felt numb physically. They had several dates and he had to summon up the courage to explain to Mandy how he felt. He said, 'I really like you a lot. I don't want you to think of this as just a friendship because it isn't that, I have plenty of friends. However, even though I would like it to carry on and perhaps develop, I have to be honest and say that even if Michelle Pfeiffer and Nicole Kidman were here right now, I would not feel like having sex with either of them.' Lucky for Barry that Mandy could see the funny side of this comment and did not take it personally (and lucky that Michelle and Nicole were not around to punch him with their Pradas). As it turned out, Mandy felt pretty much the same way. Their relationship continued for several months longer before they even kissed properly.

Barry is typical of someone in a stepping-stone relationship. He wanted to date but he needed to take it slowly. He wanted to practise all the tools he had learned with Mandy and they dated for 14 months before they both decided that they would prefer to be friends. They are still very good friends – in fact Barry introduced Mandy to his friend Roy, and they are still together as far as I know.

Stepping into Commitment
Some stepping-stone relationships can become longer term, but if they

do, they will need something of a refit. It's unlikely that you will be the same person you were when you started out in this relationship. Now the rules are changing. In order to be committed and plan for a future, you both have to be clear that your relationship is ready to move to the next level.

Happy Endings

The ultimate happy ending for many people is falling back in love again (but doing it differently this time!). If that's what you want, then that's what I want for you.

Are You Ready for Love?

To find out if you are really ready for love, I'd like you to answer the following questions with as much honesty as you can muster:

- How do you show yourself love?
- Do you believe you are lovable?
- Are you afraid of being loved in any way?
- Can you articulate what love is for you?
- Can you express your love to others in the way they want to be loved?

If you are happy with your answers and the only doubt you have about falling in love again is whether you will find the right person, then you are probably ready to fall back in love.

The Relationship Model

It's time to put everything we have talked about throughout this book into action, and for me to show you how to create a model relationship that works and can be sustained for the long term. It's the final piece of our jigsaw, and your ultimate wellness relationship tool.

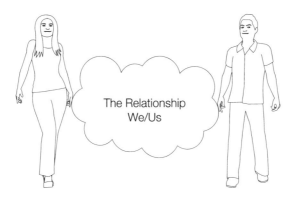

'There were three of us in this marriage, so it was a bit crowded.' – **Diana, Princess of Wales**

Our beautiful princess was right, but in this relationship model we are not talking about a third person, more a third entity. It's the space between a couple that either feels delightful or deflated. Building a sustainable relationship means having a conscious awareness of the fragility of this entity between you. It also requires a deep understanding of the many and varied components that hold it together.

When 'I' Becomes 'We'

In their effort to find the perfect partner, honour their values and stay true to themselves, many couples forget about this entity that lives between them. They are so busy concentrating on what they want for themselves, they almost forget that it's a relationship they are building – not an 'all about me' fan club.

The relationship is the place where the 'we' lives. This is the space in which the 'us' is created. A couple's job is to build a strong 'we'. This is the glue that holds them together. No 'we', no relationship. No doubt about it.

Love Is a Many-faceted Thing

Here's how an ideal relationship works. Andy and Caroline meet. When they meet they are both individuals in their own right. This means they have fulfilling jobs, have very little, if any, old baggage, they have friends, a social life and families that they love and who love them. They are, what we would call in coaching terms, creative, resourceful and whole. They don't *need* each other. They are creative enough to design their lives the way they want them to be. They are resourceful enough to take the actions that get their needs met. They don't need another person to complete them. They are whole and they are ready and able to share their lives with another person.

Magnifying Life

When two people who are perfectly capable of running their own lives and who like themselves and what they stand for meet up, the potential is there for building a lasting relationship. The whole point is not to use the relationship to fill an empty space inside yourself, but to enjoy a richer experience of life with a partner.

Magnifying the Experience

Imagine standing in front of Niagara Falls and looking in awe at its magnificence by yourself. It would be an experience you would not forget, and you would have the photos to remind you. Now imagine standing in front of Niagara Falls looking in awe at its magnificence with the person you love most in the world standing beside you. What would be the difference? It's still Niagara Falls. It's still you there enjoying the view. Why would it be better?

The answer is that looking at Niagara Falls with the perfect partner for you means that you magnify your experience by sharing it. You point out areas that catch your eye, you both marvel at its magnificence, and when you come home you share the memories which keep the experience huge for you both.

It really doesn't matter if it's watching your favourite TV programme together with a pizza and a glass of wine or travelling to the other side of the world. Being in a great relationship magnifies your experience of life through sharing it. And that's the true purpose of relationships.

And There's More

Great, so the next thing you need to know is how to make sure that you put 100 per cent of yourself into a relationship. What exactly do I mean by that?

Let's return to Andy and Caroline. In order for them to put 100 per cent of themselves into the relationship and not hold back, they will need to be able to communicate honestly and without defensiveness.

Putting in 100 per cent

To create a buoyant relationship that is sustainable over time needs conscious attention on a daily basis. This means that Andy and Caroline must be very aware of their language, their attitudes and their behaviours. The 'We' is a vulnerable entity. Everything that Caroline says to Andy and every behaviour that Andy exhibits toward Caroline, and vice versa, has to pass through the 'filter' of the relationship where the 'we' and 'us' live. At any given time, anything either of them says or does has the ability of being either relationship building or relationship destroying.

Both partners have to be careful to build a strong relationship by investing in relationship-building language and behaviours so that the relationship stays strong. Each must put in 100 per cent of their love and caring towards the other person. They must both be 'in service' of the relationship and very aware of how their language and behaviours can affect the balance and harmony of the relationship.

How to Love

The next thing Andy and Caroline need to discover is how each wants to be loved. The fact is that you cannot love someone else the way *you* would like to be loved. You have to find out how *they* want to be loved, and then honour that.

If Caroline likes to enjoy some quiet time on her own at weekends, then Andy could love her best by making it possible for her to have this. If Andy likes Caroline to come with him to cricket matches, then Caroline could love him best by going with him more often than not.

As people are not mind readers, it's sensible to let the other person know what makes you feel loved. In turn, they must let you know what makes them feel loved. The more you provide the other person with what they need, and the more they provide you with what you need, the more buoyant your 'we' becomes.

Holding on to 'I'

At the same time, Andy and Caroline must not lose sight of their individual identities. This means that they must make time for their own interests and friendships and working lives. Neither partner should feel threatened by the other's identity. Ideally each partner will be the other's greatest fan, waving them towards whatever finishing line they are aiming for and encouraging them to be the best they can be. In this way the relationship grows in strength as each partner allows the other their own personal growth. The shared 'we' grows stronger and stronger as each partner feels free to be themselves and loves the other partner for championing them.

Trying to prevent the other person from retaining their identity never works. Let me show you what I mean.

Take a look at this picture. What's the difference between this picture and the original relationship model? The answers are:

- There is no space for the relationship
- There is no individuality or identity
- Both partners are in a game of co-dependence, which is unhealthy. One is either needy or clinging to the other, or one is controlling or manipulating the other

The Relationship

Once again, what is the difference between this picture of a relationship and the original relationship model?

- The answer is that both partners have pretty much left the building.

No prizes for guessing that when a relationship is breaking down, it most resembles the second or third picture.

Why This Won't Happen to You

While all this may sound like hard work, you have to remember that the reason so many relationships fail is that most people were not given a model to work with. Believe me, it's worth putting in the time and effort if you are to create a relationship that works this time around. So let's continue.

The Spanner in the Works

It would not be real life if there were not a spanner in the works at some point, and this takes us full circle right back to where we started at the beginning of this book.

Old Wiring

The reason it all goes wrong is faulty old wiring. You'll recall that I emphasized that Andy and Caroline had to be creative, resourceful and whole individuals in order to be in a great relationship. However, if we were to pencil in their specific old wiring, above Andy's head we might write, 'I'm not appreciated.' This old wiring was born out of a childhood situation he experienced when he was about nine years old. Above Caroline's head we might write, 'I'm not loved enough,' also born out of an experience that happened when she was about seven years old.

You can probably see where this is going.

Andy leaves a wet towel on the bathroom floor. Caroline has had a hard day at work and goes to have a shower. She sees the towel on the floor and thinks, 'If Andy *loved* me he would have picked up that towel and hung it up.' She shouts down to Andy that it was pretty selfish of him to leave the towel on the floor 'once again', completely forgetting her fabulous communication skills and, in a potentially 'relationship-destroying' way, venting her frustration. Andy is preparing dinner in the kitchen and thinks that Caroline is being petty and clearly does not *appreciate* all the other things he does for her.

You can see how easy it is to fall out of love if you are not diligent in thinking about the impact you will have on the relationship if you open your mouth before engaging your brain.

Handling the Blips

Like Caroline and Andy, you will have blips in your new romance. You've learned enough by now to know how to use the right language to overcome disagreements and differences of opinion. By using your communication skills – based on your understanding of which of your values has been dishonoured in some way – you will be able to express yourself clearly to create an outcome that works for both of you.

I now have an added bonus for you, which is my 'killer line' for you to use when you need to defuse any potentially sticky situations in your new romance.

Imagine you are out on your third or fourth date and you meet up with some friends of the other person. They are pleasant enough but your new mate spends more time talking to them than you. You don't know them that well, so you feel a bit left out. You want to say something to your date but you don't want to seem clingy or needy. So you say, 'When you were talking to your friends, I felt a bit left out because I didn't feel part of the conversation. What I'd like is for you to bring me into the conversation with your friends when we are with them so I can get to know them better.' Now, here's the line: '*I'm partly responsible because …*' and then you may go on to say something like, '… I didn't tell you that I'm often shy with new people'. Then you say, '*to resolve this* in future, why not tell me a bit more about each of them so I am more prepared when we next meet.'

The beauty of this is that the other person is far more likely to be receptive and able to hear your request if they're not made to feel like it's their job to look after you. This way, no one feels blamed, guilty or attacked.

If Your Relationship Could Speak

The last word on the relationship model comes from the relationship itself. Let's imagine it has a voice all its own. If you want to check out how you are faring in your new relationship, just ask 'the relationship' how it is feeling.

Andy and Caroline both said that if their relationship could speak it would say that it really enjoys living between them and that it trusts they will always do what it takes to keep it strong. The relationship knows that Andy and Caroline fully intend to stay together for life. As they told me, their relationship was 'non-negotiable', which means that whatever obstacles they encounter, their intention was always to find a mutually agreeable solution. The voice of the relationship was relaxed and calm, and happy to stay with Andy and Caroline for as long as they kept investing in it.

You need to know that relationships can stand a bit of battering, but continuous lack of care means they will pack up and leave if you don't reinvest in them. Take care of your relationship and it will take care of you. I promise.

Finally ...

... Learning to Love Again

Divorce can be an earth-shattering experience, but it can also be the greatest growth-enhancing event of your life. Your heart has mended and you are ready to open it up again to love. Everything we have talked about in this book is designed to lead you down a healing path towards restored health and wellness. I cannot guarantee that you will never be hurt again. I cannot guarantee that if you risk opening your heart, someone may not find some old wounds that have not properly healed and you may experience some pain again. But I can guarantee that you will survive.

We are born to love. It is our birthright and I know that you are now armed with the right tools and skills to help you heal your heart, regain your identity, stay buoyant, not bitter, and learn to love again. One day we may meet and you can tell me how you overcame your obstacles and built your new life. I send you all my love and wish you a wonderful future.

Resources

Personal Support

I have helped hundreds of couples and individuals rehabilitate their relationships or divorce with dignity. If you would like to work with me to address your personal circumstances in a safe and confidential environment, get in touch with me at Francine@thedivorcedoctor.com. You can also visit my website at www.thedivorcedoctor.com and subscribe to my newsletter and receive monthly advice from my team of advisers or take advantage of my free online mini-series.

The Divorce Support Group

If you'd like to join a group to learn new skills and receive the support of other members at an affordable price, go to www.thedivorcesupportgroup.com for information about groups in your area.

Parenting Apart Groups

Parenting Apart is challenging for most people. This six-week or weekend course provides cutting edge skills and strategies so you can communicate effectively with your children, create more trust, understanding, acceptance and positive regard as well as confidence and insight into your children's behaviour after divorce. Parents report that their children have fewer tantrums and emotional scenes; exhibit increased self-esteem, become more open to parents' influence and often improve their school performance. Parents themselves are more relaxed, less stressed and are able to manage conflicts between ex-partners and children so that everyone's needs are satisfied.

Go to www.parentingapart.co.uk for details of groups in your area.

Here are some of my personally recommended support services:

Andrew Rhodes – Sobell Rhodes Accountants. Andrew Rhodes is a person of the highest integrity and someone I absolutely trust. He is not just an ordinary accountant, but someone who takes the time to understand life from your perspective. I would highly recommend his services to anyone who needs expert financial advice during and after the divorce process. Take a moment to visit Sobell Rhodes site, or better still, call him for a confidential chat. www.sobellrhodes.co.uk

Amanda Burnstein – Amanda is an image maker and one of the UK's top stylists and fashion journalists. She has helped hundreds of men and women revamp their wardrobes, update their appearance and learn to dress in a way that represents who they are right now. Amanda recently 'dressed' one of my best and dearest friends after her divorce and gave her back her confidence and a subtle sexiness that her new man absolutely loves. Amanda's warmth and enthusiasm is wonderful and her skill totally priceless. She is available by appointment and for a preliminary chat. Just visit her at www.personaldressing.com

Vanessa Lloyd Platt – Vanessa is one of the top family lawyers in London. She is simply the most compassionate and understanding lawyer I have met. Vanessa and her partners undertake all kinds of matrimonial and divorce work and have represented many celebrities from the world of TV, radio and entertainment, as well as judges and MPs. However you certainly don't have to be a celebrity to have her experienced support with your divorce. Her caring approach to clients from all walks of life is what makes the firm of Lloyd Platt & Company stand out from the rest. Before you decide on legal representation, I would highly recommend you speak to Vanessa and find out how she can help you. www.divorcesoliticors.com

Recommended Reading

Be Your Own Life Coach by Fiona Harrold

Change Your Thoughts, Change Your Life by Dr Wayne Dyer

Eat Pray Love by Elizabeth Gilbert

How to Mend your Broken Heart by Paul McKenna

The Legacy of Divorce by Julia M. Lewis and Sandra Blakeslee

Manhood by Steve Biddulph

More than Money by Grainne O'Malley

Raising Boys by Steve Biddulph

Rebuilding When Your Relationship Ends by Dr Bruce Fisher and
    Dr Robert Alberti

Time to Live by Francine Kaye

When Divorce Hits Home by Beth Joselow and Thea Joselow

The Which Guide to Divorce by Imogen Clout

Women Who Love Too Much by Robin Norwood

You Can Excel in Times of Change by Shad Helmstetter

You Can Heal Your Life by Louise L. Hay

To name but a few!

NOTES

NOTES

NOTES

NOTES

NOTES

NOTES

NOTES

HAY HOUSE PUBLISHERS

For the most up-to-date
information on the
latest releases, author
appearances and a host
of special offers, visit

www.hayhouse.co.uk

Tune into **www.hayhouseradio.com**
to hear inspiring live radio shows daily!

292B Kensal Rd, London W10 5BE
Tel: 020 8962 1230 Email: info@hayhouse.co.uk

We hope you enjoyed this Hay House book.
If you would like to receive a free catalogue featuring additional
Hay House books and products, or if you would like information
about the Hay Foundation, please contact:

Hay House UK Ltd
292B Kensal Rd • London W10 5BE
Tel: (44) 20 8962 1230; Fax: (44) 20 8962 1239
www.hayhouse.co.uk

***

Published and distributed in the United States of America by:
Hay House, Inc. • PO Box 5100 • Carlsbad, CA 92018-5100
Tel.: (1) 760 431 7695 or (1) 800 654 5126;
Fax: (1) 760 431 6948 or (1) 800 650 5115
www.hayhouse.com

Published and distributed in Australia by:
Hay House Australia Ltd • 18/36 Ralph St • Alexandria NSW 2015
Tel.: (61) 2 9669 4299; Fax: (61) 2 9669 4144
www.hayhouse.com.au

Published and distributed in the Republic of South Africa by:
Hay House SA (Pty) Ltd • PO Box 990 • Witkoppen 2068
Tel./Fax: (27) 11 467 8904 • www.hayhouse.co.za

Published and distributed in India by:
Hay House Publishers India • Muskaan Complex • Plot No.3
B-2 • Vasant Kunj • New Delhi – 110 070.
Tel.: (91) 11 41761620; Fax: (91) 11 41761630.
www.hayhouse.co.in

Distributed in Canada by:
Raincoast • 9050 Shaughnessy St • Vancouver, BC V6P 6E5
Tel.: (1) 604 323 7100; Fax: (1) 604 323 2600

***

Sign up via the Hay House UK website to receive the Hay House
online newsletter and stay informed about what's going on with
your favourite authors. You'll receive bimonthly announcements
about discounts and offers, special events, product highlights,
free excerpts, giveaways, and more!
www.hayhouse.co.uk